AMONG THE REEDS

THE TRUE STORY OF HOW A FAMILY SURVIVED THE HOLOCAUST

TAMMY BOTTNER

ISBN 9789492371294 (ebook)

ISBN 9789492371287 (paperback)

ISBN 9789493231221 (audio)

Publisher: Amsterdam Publishers, The Netherlands

info@amsterdampublishers.com

Among the Reeds. The true story of how a family survived the Holocaust is part of the series Holocaust Survivor True Stories WWII

Cover photo: Genek, Melly, Irene, and Bobby, after the war, c. 1946

CONTENTS

I dedicate this book to those who survived:

To my Dad, Al (Bobby) Bottner, and my Aunt Irene, whose childhoods were snatched from them too soon, and to Uncle Nathan, Aunt Shoshana, and Aunt Inge, for their remarkable resilience. And especially to my grandparents Melly and Genek, who had the courage to make unthinkable choices.

The world can finally hear your story.

And also to the six million lost souls whose stories will never be told.

But when she could no longer hide him, she got a basket made of papyrus reeds and waterproofed it with tar and pitch. She put the baby in the basket and laid it among the reeds along the bank of the Nile River. - Exodus 2:3

Who has fully realized that history is not contained in thick books but lives in our very blood? - Carl Jung

ACKNOWLEDGMENTS

A huge thank you to everyone who encouraged and supported me through the process of researching and writing this book.

Thank you to Liesbeth Heenk at Amsterdam Publishers for your enthusiastic response to publishing this story, and to Luke Finley for your careful and thoughtful editing.

To my friends – thank you for cheering me on. I appreciate each of you tremendously. To my family, especially Sharon, who read early versions and provided helpful advice. Special thanks to my wonderful husband Danny, without whose support in writing and in life I would be lost. And to my kids, Ari and Sophia – it's always for you.

PROLOGUE
TAMMY, NEWBURYPORT, MASSACHUSETTS

It was the spring of 1997, and I had a newborn baby. He had arrived ten days after his due date, pronounced healthy, and after four days at Newton Wellesley Hospital his father and I drove him home, me sitting beside him in the backseat because, like every new mother, I was worried he would stop breathing back there and who would know? But I only did that the one time, then I sat up front like a normal person, confident Ari would survive the car ride. I really was not an overly anxious new mother. As a pediatrician I had more experience than most new moms. I could see Ari was a strong and robust baby.

We had just moved into a little carriage house in Newburyport, and had fixed up the smallest bedroom as a nursery. Ari's room held a light-colored wooden crib and changing table and a pretty lamp his aunt had painted for him, and sported a good-sized window which looked out onto a leafy street. Danny was working as a psychiatrist in a local practice, and I had four months' leave before I would be starting work in a pediatric practice. We were newly settled in a lovely community. Everything was good.

Yet I was terrified. And I don't mean just the regular "oh my God I have a newborn what do I do" type of terrified. I had already taken care of hundreds of newborn babies, many of them premature or sick. Feeding and caring for my sturdy little son was not difficult for me. My husband, Danny, was a bit scared in that way, but for me even the waking up at night to feed baby Ari was a cakewalk compared to the stress-filled, sleep-deprived years of my residency.

No, I was terrified because I was caught in a waking dream, that of a parallel universe, one in which I had given birth in a different time and place, in which an unspeakable horror was in store for me and for my child.

My grandparents were Holocaust survivors. My father, too, was a survivor. He had lived through World War Two as a young child in Europe. Despite the thousands of miles and more than fifty years of time separating my family's traumatic wartime experiences from that of Ari's birth, I found myself reliving the trauma. It was deeply troubling and very strange.

When I was a young girl, we would sometimes drive up to Montreal to visit my father's parents, whom I called Boma and Saba. The adults would put my sister and me to bed and then stay up talking about "the war". But of course I was still awake, and listening, and could hear all kinds of scary things. Since I wasn't supposed to be listening, I never spoke about these late-night reminiscences. But the fear they elicited stayed deep inside me. I can't even remember any specifics of what I heard now, but I can very clearly recall lying in bed with my heart pounding, experiencing equal parts guilt for not having had to suffer as they had, and horror at what they went through.

Decades later, while I was pregnant with Ari, Danny and I watched the Holocaust movie Schindler's List. It was awful. Of course, I knew about the horrors of the Holocaust. I had read plenty of books, heard lots of stories, some even first hand. But this movie somehow clarified the degradation, the humiliation, the slavery, and the pointless sadism that the Jews endured under the Nazis. The movie struck a deep cord in me. For days afterward I couldn't sleep, images of the movie haunting my imagination, a feeling of fear permeating my being so completely that I didn't know what to do. But slowly I returned to normal, and I thought I had moved past the reaction the movie had caused me.

When Ari was born, however, those feelings came back. Even as I looked around my little house in beautiful Newburyport, part of me was living in Nazi-occupied Europe during World War Two. Profound terror shook me as I gazed at my baby boy lying in his bassinet beside me, and obsessive thoughts went through my mind – what if we were being hunted? What if boots were pounding up the stairs to our room? Where would I hide? What would I do if he cried? What if I had to give him up in order to save his life?

Was it just because of what I had heard as a child that I experienced this terrible distress? Maybe. But perhaps – and I mean this literally – the horror of the Holocaust was actually in my DNA.

Epigenetics is a relatively new scientific field, but a fascinating one. We used to believe that our genes, which we inherit from our parents at conception, formed a permanent and unchanging blueprint of our makeup for our entire lives. In other words, you got what you got, and that was it forever. We now know that it's a lot more complicated. It seems to be true that genes themselves don't change, but what is incredible is that there are countless ways that the expression of these genes is changeable. And almost everything we do, eat, or experience in life can change the way our genes are expressed.

So, it is possible that the trauma that my grandparents lived through, and that my father experienced as a child, actually changed their genes, and that these altered genes were passed on to me. If I inherited some of the trauma of the Holocaust in my very genes, maybe that explains my visceral reaction to seeing Schindler's List and other Holocaust movies, and my overwhelming anxiety when Ari was born.

My family's plight during World War Two was a story deeply rooted in my psyche. I thought a lot about it, and at the same time couldn't bear to consider it. The whole thing was too terrible, too intense. In fact, for years I tried to avoid all things Holocaust-related once I realized that seeing movies or reading books about the subject elicited anxiety, sleeplessness, and a strange kind of post-traumatic stress disorder (PTSD) in me. It was only recently that I summoned the courage to interview my relatives and to fully imagine what they went through.

My father did not talk about his childhood experiences with my sister and me until we were adults. When he did finally divulge what had occurred, he insisted that he had previously told us, that we had already heard these stories. My guess is that his history was so prominent in his own psyche that he couldn't imagine that we weren't aware of it. I think of it like being in a loud concert hall, and having to explain to someone beside you that there is actually music playing. How could you not be aware?

As he got older my dad spoke more openly about his World War Two experiences. Once he retired, he spent about a decade giving regular talks to high-school students about the Holocaust, and about his story in particular. He felt, I think, that he was honoring the memories of those who were lost by giving these talks. Eventually, though, he too realized that the memories exacted a price: he found he was having nightmares and flashbacks after these lectures, and so he stopped.

But he wanted to tell his story. He thought about writing it down, but he is an engineer; his skills are more analytical than verbal and, while his English is excellent, still it is not his first language. The task seemed daunting. He spoke to me about hiring a ghostwriter. I started thinking that maybe I would do it. The more I considered it, the more I realized that I very much wanted to research what had happened and to put it together into a book. I felt very drawn to the tale; the story was mine as much as anyone's.

This was not the first time a family member had mentioned the idea of writing down this incredible story. When I was in college, my grandmother Melly – Boma – mentioned that she would like to write a book about her life. As I recall, she thought for a moment and then said, you know, Tammeleh, I should tell you my story, and you should write the book. She had shared a few anecdotes with me, but there was a lot I didn't know. Unfortunately, she passed away soon after, and I never had the opportunity to interview her and to obtain her complete story first hand. But her voice remained in my head, and as I embarked on creating this book I realized I had to tell at least some of it from her point of view. Sadly, it was also too late to interview my grandfather Genek; he too had passed away, years earlier.

Although I got a lot of information from my father, I realized it was important to interview as many other key players in the story as possible. In May 2016 I flew to Israel, and spent a wonderful week with my dad's sister, my Aunt Irene, and her husband, Uncle Shlomo. I spoke to Irene at length about her memories, her parents, and her childhood. We pored over old photos and memorabilia, piecing together as much information as we could. I also visited my Great-Uncle Nathan. Still sharp as ever at eighty-eight, he astounded me with his remarkable memory for names, dates, and addresses. I talked to Nathan for hours, taping the conversation so I could review it later. Also I met with Inge's son, my wonderful cousin Ami. Two of Ami's own sons, Omri and Gilad, came to see me too; they all were eager to tell me what they knew about their mother's and grandmother's stories.

When I got back to the U.S. I started researching the many places where my family's story had taken place. I studied about hidden children. I learned World War Two history. I ordered books, I read articles, I watched documentaries. But still, it was not possible to know everything that had happened seventy, even eighty years prior with complete accuracy. I knew the facts – where people were born, when they moved, where they lived. I learned the historic context. I could verify the major events that my relatives described. Whenever possible I verified the facts with my dad, or with my great-uncle Nathan, via Skype.

An additional challenge was that I discovered that many of my Jewish ancestors went by several different names. Known to the family by their Jewish name, they might be formally registered by a secular name, and perhaps referred to by most people by a nickname. For example, I found that my paternal great-grandfather Yehudah Bottner was registered in the Lvov phone book as Ignacy Bottner. My great-grandmother Beila sent a telegram signed Berta Bottner. My grandfather Genek was actually named Gimpel. And so on.

So I had a lot of information. But in order to write this book I had to take a few liberties. I had to imagine myself as my grandmother, as my grandfather, as my father, as each of the characters in the story, and to learn what they were likely thinking as best I could. Sometimes this was difficult, but mostly it wasn't. I knew the characters well – as their older incarnations of course, but I did know them first hand. And the more I wrote, the more immersed I became in the story, the more I found that what had seemed to be odd, disjointed facts suddenly seemed to make more sense. Oh, I would think, that happened, and that must be why that other thing happened. And the timing of that makes sense, and that jibes with what was going on in that place at that time. At times I felt like a sleuth, piecing together bits of history with family anecdotes.

So how accurate is this book? So much of what occurred is lost, this long afterward. All the major occurrences happened in the way I describe, as told to me by family members. The historical parts of the book are true and verifiable. Much of the story is based on the memories of primary sources. Sometimes two relatives remember things a bit differently from each other, as is the way with memories. I have done my best to synthesize the information, and have added some plausible details that I have surmised are true, but do not know for sure. So my answer is that it is a true story, gleaned from first-hand accounts and from research. It is as accurate as I can realistically be, with just a dash of poetic license, and if I got some things wrong, I apologize. My intention is to recount a remarkable tale, to share that story with the world, and to preserve it for the future. To that end I have done the best I could.

THE OFFNER-BOTTNER FAMILY TREE

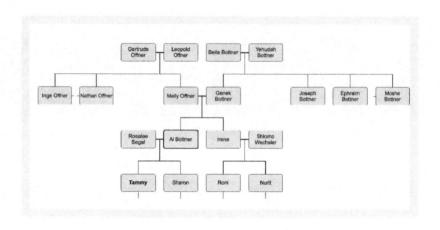

MELLY
GERMANY, 1920S AND 1930S

I was a disappointment to my father from the day I was born, September 30, 1921. My parents were in transit at the time of my birth, having fled from their native country, war-torn Poland, in the bloody wake of World War One. Mama and Papa, Gertrude and Leopold Offner, newlywed Jews, were searching for a better place to live. They headed into what was then a place of relative enlightenment, the neighboring country, Germany. Mama was already carrying me in her womb.

The year of my birth was one of transitions. I was born during a stopover when my mother went into labor just over the border in the German city of Leignitz. So I became a German citizen at birth. Years later Germany would strip me of this citizenship, of course – in Nazi Germany, Jews' citizenship was taken away. In Nazi Germany, Jews' everything was taken away. But that was later...

September 30 should have been a joyous day, when Leopold and Gertrude became new parents. But Leopold was not a happy man, and he was not pleased to hear he had a little girl; he wanted a son.

And maybe that early failure was imprinted on me, for hardship, disappointment, and heartbreak were to dog me, sadness to permeate my soul. It's a fitting metaphor, I think, that my Jewish parents fled a difficult life to settle in Germany of all places. So things were not destined to turn out well. I'd have liked to have been born an optimist. It would be wonderful, I think, to have a sunny disposition, to see the world gently, view life as a cornucopia of opportunity. My sister Inge is like that, a sweet soul, God love her. But me, no. My motto is schver bitter leiben, it's a hard and bitter life, because mostly that's how it has been. But I was tough, born on the run, and destined to keep moving all my life. Fate dealt me some bad hands, but I fought back with all the grit and brains and determination I had in me.

My father Leopold was born on October 21, 1887, in Oświęcim, Poland – the town known in German as Auschwitz. Can you imagine? He was born in the town that would later house the most notorious killing camp of the war. Fifty-six years later he would die there. I warned you that this was not a happy story. Leopold was the second of seven children, five boys, two girls. People had big families in those days. This was before antibiotics, before immunizations, in the days when a routine sore throat or a small cut could lead to overwhelming infection and death. People had a lot of children, but not all of them survived. Infant mortality was appallingly high.

My parents were both raised in Orthodox Jewish families. Things were different then: Jews and non-Jews didn't mix much. Jews had their own neighborhoods, their own schools, their own stores. Men and women were more segregated too; each gender had prescribed roles, women keeping a kosher home, cooking, cleaning, sewing, and raising children, men working to make a living and studying and praying in synagogue as many hours as they possibly could.

Everyone they knew spoke Yiddish, a colorful hybrid of German with a smattering of Hebrew, Aramaic, Latin, and Slavic roots, but written in the Hebrew alphabet. Jews had a hard life in Poland. Antisemitism was rampant, and pogroms regularly terrorized the Jewish community, as gangs of hoodlums took to the streets, looting businesses, and beating, even killing, any Jews they could find.

In 1914 World War One broke out across Europe, and my father was conscripted to serve in the Austrian army, as Poland was then part of the Austrian-Hungarian Empire. Yes, my Orthodox Jewish father, later to be killed at Auschwitz, fought for the "other side" during World War One. Lots of Polish Jews fought during the Great War, defending the countries that would turn on them a couple of decades later. Jewish boys weren't good for much in Poland, but they were tolerable as cannon fodder for the front lines.

I don't know how much good a yeshivah boy would have been at fighting. Papa probably tried to keep his head down as much as possible. Jewish soldiers had double trouble. Not only did they have to slog through the mud, enduring the horror of trench warfare like everyone else, they also had to put up with the harassment of their antisemitic fellow troops. A lot of those Jewish soldiers were killed by their own side. It was a national pastime to harass the Jews, and in war conditions, with hunger and cold and depravity and guns – well, it doesn't take much effort to imagine the terrible ends some of those kids came to.

But Leopold was a survivor. He realized his chances of coming out of the Great War alive were slim. If a French bullet didn't take him out, if disease didn't claim him, if gangrene didn't set into his sodden feet, he might well be beaten to death by a fellow Pole. So he weighed his options.

In a bold and terrible move, he made a decision. He decided to instill poison drops into his eyes. I don't know exactly what he used

– he called the drops seedit or seedim. He told us years later that desperate soldiers knew how to get a hold of the stuff, and took their chances with blindness over certain death by cannon. He put those terrible poison drops into his own eyes. He must have suffered terribly, but the result was sufficient to obtain a medical discharge from the army. Papa wasn't exactly blind after that, but he couldn't see very well for the rest of his life. Like I said, he was a tough man.

And so Leopold survived the Great War, and in 1919 he and my mother Gertrude were married in Poland. They didn't tell me details of their betrothal – parents didn't discuss personal details with their children in my home – but I'm sure theirs must have been an arranged marriage. That was the custom. A shidduch, a matchmaker, would have gone between the families and made the arrangements. Marriage was a big deal, a mitzvah, a fulfillment of a promise to God to be fruitful and multiply.

Parents, especially fathers, made sure the young people were matched in various categories: how observant they were of Jewish traditions and customs, the economic status of their families, the education and potential of the man, the morality of the woman. There were financial considerations too – a dowry to negotiate, as well as wedding presents to get the young couple set up in their independent life. I wonder whether my parents ever spent an hour alone together before their wedding night. I doubt it. And that reminds me of my own marriage. But I'm getting ahead of myself.

Jewish weddings were traditional, with a rabbi performing an ancient Hebrew service as the couple stood under the chuppah, or wedding canopy. Afterward, a party, but segregated by gender – men dancing with men, women doing the horah in an adjoining area, gossiping and giggling separately from the men.

I wonder how my mother felt about her groom. At age twenty-five she was relatively old to arrive at the chuppah, but the war had interrupted the normal flow of life, and all the eligible young men who survived had only just returned from the front. And so she embarked on married life with Leopold, a 32-year-old man hardened by war, partially blind, fiercely intelligent, ambitious, a survivor. Not an affectionate man, her new husband, but determined and strong, tall, stern, with eerie eyes in his shaved, well-shaped head.

My mother, Gertrude Fischer, was lovely, with softly curling brown hair that she wore in a chignon, a small straight nose, and gray eyes. Like all Jewish girls, she was raised to be a balebusteh, a dedicated home-maker, keeping a tidy house, cooking for the family, and baking delicious pastries, cakes, and breads. On Fridays before Shabbos she worked tirelessly, scrubbing the floors, setting the table and preparing the chicken liver, matza ball soup, roast chicken, challah, and a platter of desserts.

Mama was the second of nine siblings, born in Sosnowietz, Poland, on October 28, 1894. Hers was a large and close family, and in fact, many of her brothers and sisters ended up leaving Poland around the same time my parents did, and settling near us in Germany. So I knew my Tantes and Onkels during my growing up years later. Because Mama was one of the eldest siblings, some of my Tantes were so close to me in age that I thought of them as cousins.

When I was still a baby Mama and Papa continued their journey, settling in the city of Chemnitz, where I grew up and where my siblings were eventually born, Inge in 1924 and Nathan – finally, a son! – in 1928.

Chemnitz was a big city at that time, with about three hundred thousand inhabitants. It is located in what would later be called East Germany, in Saxony, about fifty miles from Dresden. It was beautiful despite being a thriving industrial center. The buildings were ornate, with pointy roofs, and the Chemnitz River ran through town. The city boasted elegant plazas surrounded by gothic spires. The Ore Mountains were visible from upper balconies.

There was a thriving Jewish community in Chemnitz at that time, with about 2,400 Jews living in the city. My family was one of the typical Jewish transplants who had made their way there from Eastern Europe after the Great War. There were various Jewish organizations in town, Jewish schools, and even a mikvah. I remember there was a Jewish newspaper, the Jüdische Zeitung für Mittelsachsen, that my father would wait for eagerly every month. The Old Synagogue on Stephansplatz had been built before the turn of the century. It was an imposing Romanesque building with a cupola, enormous turrets, arched doorways, tiled roofs, and a gorgeous round window facing the street. It could hold 700 people. That famous synagogue was eventually destroyed, of course. It was attacked on Kristallnacht, on November 9, 1938, as were so many Jewish businesses in town. But that was much later.

Textiles had been produced in Chemnitz since the Middle Ages, and after the industrial revolution the area continued to be a center for spinning and production of various fabrics. Leopold was a businessman, and he chose to live in Chemnitz because it was a center for textile production. His company made gloves and socks, and I guess people needed a lot of gloves and socks during those years, because business was very good, and our family prospered.

Our first house in Chemnitz was at Glockenstrasse 2. This house was in downtown Chemnitz, on a lovely street of five-story attached homes, built of stone, and painted in warm colors, with balconies on the upper floors. But after a few years, as my family's business prospered, we moved to a larger house.

As our finances improved, my family hired servants and a governess; we even acquired an automobile when I was a toddler. I know this because I remember falling out of that car once, when I was about two, and I have a scar as a souvenir. Later, when we were destitute, reminiscing about those years of plenty, they seemed like a fairy tale, a dream. I mean, to think we had the money to afford a car in Germany in 1923!

Not that my childhood was easy, or even pleasant. My father was extremely hard on me, and my mother was unable to protect me from his exacting standards, or from his wrath. Until my brother Nathan was born, Leopold insisted that I, his eldest daughter, shoulder the Jewish traditions he believed in so strongly. In addition to regular school, my father insisted that I study Hebrew and Torah like a boy. Personally, I never cared for religious life, but that was irrelevant. If I complained I was whipped.

Many Jews who emigrated to Germany around this time abandoned the Orthodox religion of their homeland, assimilating into the secular goyishe German society. The world was changing, and people were embracing a more modern way of life. Not so my father. Ironically, he became ever more observant as the years went by, almost fanatical. Maybe his mind was already starting to slip, his religiosity an early sign of the madness that was to come.

All I knew was that Papa forced me to study like a boy, and I was terribly resentful of the burden he placed on me. I became the surrogate son – studying Torah – but also was forced to play the role of the perfect daughter, taking ballet lessons, and learning how to keep a home. My family was economically privileged, but I did not have the privilege of free time, or of free choice for that matter.

And while school came easily to me, and I was naturally gifted in cooking and baking, and loved to knit – I found knitting very soothing, and it gave me a creative outlet to design complicated patterns in my sweaters – I always felt awkward with the ballet lessons. I was not built like a ballerina, with my knock-knees and my pudgy thighs. But you see, I had no choice, so ballet it was.

When I was three years old my sister Inge was born. Despite loving my younger sister, I sometimes mistreated her, maybe taking out on her the resentment I was not allowed to express toward my father. Inge was a lovely soul, the gentlest of children. Despite that, I teased her mercilessly, telling her she wasn't really part of the family, that our parents had found her on the street and adopted her. I told her the rest of us had blue eyes, and hers were brown, because she wasn't related to us. Poor Inge was no match for my sharp tongue, and it is with shame that I admit I caused her terrible pain. When she ran off crying I felt no sorrow. Children's cruelty can be astonishing.

During the years before the Nazis came to power, despite the tyranny at home, life was as normal for my family as it would ever be. My many aunts and uncles lived either in Chemnitz or nearby, and we had frequent visitors to our lovely new home at Postrasse 1, located west of downtown Chemnitz. This home was a free-standing house, different from the inner city attached home we had lived in previously. We had a leafy yard, and lovely views of the lush countryside. Still, I sort of missed living downtown so close to all the stores and cafes.

I remember so many Shabbos dinners around our grand dining table, the white tablecloth, the polished silver, and candles reflecting on Tante Rozel and Tante Anna's bright eyes, Uncle Herman mischievously kicking my leg under the table, trying to get me in trouble. Inge smiling shyly at the guests in her sweet way.

I should mention that although my parents' first language was Yiddish we spoke German at home. My father insisted his family be well educated, and the shtetl Yiddish was not to his liking. Our governess and tutors schooled my siblings and myself in the posh German of the upper classes. Little did I know that this linguistic ability would help save my life someday.

In 1928 my father's dream of having a son was finally realized when Nathan was born. Nathan was Leopold's darling child, and I was both relieved that a boy had arrived and resentful of the obvious favoritism he inspired. Nathan was a beautiful child, with big blue eyes, and as he got old enough, I recruited him in my persecution of poor Inge.

We were cruel to Inge as children are, but we really didn't know how much we hurt her until later. I guess our constant teasing and taunts really did a number on her. One day when she was about nine years old, my mother found her standing on a kitchen stool with a belt around her neck. Inge was planning to hang herself! My mother's screams still ring in my ears to this day. She managed to reach Inge in time, but the horror of what almost happened stayed with all of us for the rest of our lives. I was whipped for the part I played in making Inge miserable, further fueling my resentment against my father. But I really was sorry. I was more careful with Inge after that.

Most people aren't even aware that another war took place between Russia and Poland after World War One ended. The Bolshevik Russians were trying to establish a communist regime in the area, while Poland was desperately fighting to stay independent. Fierce clashes took place between the Red Army and the Polish army, in a country already ravaged by the Great War. In the aftermath of World War One, Poland was a place of upheaval and uncertainty.

Desperate people like my parents streamed out of the area, heading west, into Germany and beyond, searching for a better life. Most of them came by foot or horse-drawn buggy, carrying sacks of belongings, destitute, with children alongside and babies strapped to their mothers' backs. Some of these refugees were Jews from the towns my parents had grown up in.

My father became very involved in helping these Jewish refugees from Poland. By this time he was well established financially, and able to offer assistance to the desperate families that came through Chemnitz. I remember late-night meetings at my house, candles flickering, reflecting on the worry-lined faces of the men gathered in the back parlor, whispering frantically in Yiddish. I understood enough to realize there was danger in having these people here, although it was not my place to ask questions.

Sometimes the refugees stayed with us for a few days or weeks until they came up with a more permanent plan. My father acted as a liaison, made introductions, helped the men find employment. My mother fed and clothed the endless stream of impoverished Jews flowing through our home.

It was being involved with these refugees that made my father a suspect when the National Socialist party came into power in Germany in 1933. Hitler's Nazis hated a lot of people, but in the early days of their power they especially hated communists. And housing and helping people from the Russian/Polish bloc brought my father under Nazi suspicion immediately. At least my father thought so; but Papa was becoming increasingly suspicious and strange. Maybe those poison drops he put in his eyes during the war did something to his brain, I don't know. At any rate, it wasn't clear to me at the time whether the Nazis really were observing us or whether that was a figment of Papa's active imagination.

Like everyone, we were wary of the Nazi party, astonished that Hitler was being welcomed by the German people, but hoping that he would soon be ousted. Our adopted country was a civilized one, known for its music, its literature, its scholars. Hitler was an anomaly, a temporary madness; the German people would soon realize he was a madman, surely. Germany was much too cultured to harbor a leader who spouted hate, shouting and madly gesticulating and throwing his arm up in the air! Still, it was very upsetting to see his rallies attracting ever larger crowds. And soon his rhetoric scared the daylights out of me. The way he demonized us Jews, blaming us for Germany's economic woes, painting us as thieves and villains. We had to hope that this madness was temporary.

I desperately hoped Papa was being paranoid, because having the Nazis scrutinize him, observing our family, seemed terrible, terrifying. The worst possible thing. Papa may well have been paranoid. But maybe that was the first of many pieces of bizarre luck, strange little fragments that came together like a macabre jigsaw puzzle, piecing our family's story together during those years of war.

As I said, I am not an optimist. But even I have to admit that some of the terrible things that happened to us may have saved our lives. It's strange. At the time you have no idea. But later, looking back, you realize – if that hadn't happened, and that hadn't happened, maybe we wouldn't have left, and if we hadn't done that, and that, well...

At any rate, I will never forget the March morning in 1933, just weeks after the Nazis came to power in Germany, when Papa left home. Mama said he woke up that morning in a terrible state. He had dreamt that the S.R., the brown shirts, the most sinister of the Nazi soldiers, were coming for him. Mama tried to reason with him, saying it was only a dream. There was no rush, no reason to run off without a well thought-out plan. What was she to do? What about the house, the children, the servants? And the business? But Papa was adamant. The S.R. were coming, and he was leaving, immediately.

Papa packed a small satchel and disappeared toward the railway station. He was leaving Chemnitz, leaving Germany, taking the train to Holland. He would be in touch with Mama presently and we were to wait until we heard from him. We children, Mama, and the servants stood at the window and watched him walk down the street. I don't remember what I felt. I expected him to be back in a couple of days, I suppose.

These S.R. stormtroopers Papa referred to, who seemed to have sprung up on every street corner overnight, were indeed terrifying. With their shiny knee-high boots, brown-belted uniforms, and red armbands imprinted with the swastika, their goose-stepping marches around the city frightened everyone. We knew they hated communists and Jews, but we didn't yet feel vulnerable. Our father was a successful businessman, and we were respected citizens in the community. It wasn't until much later that we would realize the single-minded hate and brutality that the Nazis would direct toward our people.

Remember, this was March 1933. The Nazis had only come into power two months earlier. Most Jews, and non-Jews for that matter, were unhappy about Hitler's rise, but not overly alarmed. Most people in our circle considered him a charlatan, an ignorant bumpkin, who would soon be exposed for the fool that he was and would disappear from public life. We had no way of knowing, no-one did, that he would become the all-powerful dictator of Germany; no-one could foresee the madness that was to come. In those early days one could easily leave the country; it was still the Weimar Republic, a fractured but democratic state. Even Jews could leave; in fact, as the Nazis slowly increased control of the country in the 1930s, Jews were encouraged to leave. The borders were open, trains were running, and people were coming and going. There were soldiers and stormtroopers around, yes, and they were starting to demand identification papers, but getting out was not a problem at all.

And so Papa left for Holland because he had a dream, a premonition, that he was in danger. We didn't yet know it, but our privileged life as German citizens had just ended. I was eleven years old.

And just two or three days after Papa's departure we awoke to hear a furious pounding at the front door. It was loud, shocking. Our home was a place of quiet voices, of restraint. I will never forget the two Nazi stormtroopers who stomped into the house demanding to see Leopold Offner. The soldiers were tall and imposing, and I remember my shock at hearing their crude German and disrespectful tone. I had never heard my mother addressed this way. Inge hid behind Mama's skirts, whimpering, and Nathan flew into the governess's arms. I stood by the stairs, partially hidden, watching as Mama explained that Herr Offner was not home, and that she didn't expect him back for some time. The S.R. soldiers were enraged. They accused Mama of lying. Brandishing bayonets at the ends of their rifles, they stormed from room to room searching for Papa, tearing into closets, throwing our belongings on the floor, stabbing sofas and mattresses with their steely blades. Their boots left muddy prints on Mama's beautiful rugs. By then we were all crying.

Eventually, after what seemed like hours, they must have realized Papa was indeed not in the house. The sterner of the two, the leader I suppose, informed Mama that we were now under house arrest, confined to our home, forbidden to leave. They would keep our family hostage until Papa's return. Their commander had demanded Leopold Offner's arrest, and they would make sure that Leopold Offner was delivered to him. There would be a soldier posted outside our door to ensure that we complied. If we disobeyed we would be dealt with harshly. Heil Hitler! The door slammed behind them.

Hours later, when I summoned the courage to take a peek out the window, I saw that indeed a tall blond S.R. soldier wearing that shiny uniform stood guard at our front door, barring the exit. His gun glinted in the weak March sunlight.

For all Mama's gentle demeanor, she had incredible strength. Rather than fall apart, she dried her tears, put on a brave face, and immediately started organizing the family. First she dismissed the servants for the day. Our governess, who was not Jewish by the way, chose to remain with us children. The rest of the help fled the house as quickly as they could. We never saw any of them again. Mama next bade the governess take us kids to the nursery so she could make plans. I resisted. At eleven I felt like I didn't belong with the little children. Mama, worn out, I think, by the events of the day, and likely relieved to have an assistant, relented. And so I remained by her side, helping her "get ready," she said. I wasn't sure what we were doing, really, but I preferred to be part of the action rather than banished to the nursery.

Mama brought me into her dressing room, drew the curtains, and locked the door. She started collecting photographs and other small items that she cherished, placing them carefully into a small sack.

I don't know if I dreamt the rest or if it actually happened. Maybe I saw this, maybe I just surmised it when I looked back on this day years later. But as I recall she gathered a few dresses and ripped open the seams, carefully inserting her best pieces of jewelry into the folds and sewing the seams back up. I do remember her insisting that everything I saw was a secret. It's for security, she told me. Do not tell anyone about this. I understood we were hiding valuables because we were in danger. I definitely remember that much.

The next morning Mama told us we too were leaving. We would make our way through the back door. Quietly, carefully, and not all together.

Don't be afraid, children, she told us. You girls know your way to the train station. It isn't safe for us to go together, so listen carefully to what we have to do.

The Nazis had posted a guard to keep us under house arrest, but he was only guarding the front door. I guess they didn't know we had a back door. Later on those Nazi bastards would have been more thorough, more compulsive, and there would have been no chance of us walking out the back way. But that is exactly what we did.

First Mama instructed the governess to escort five-year-old Nathan out. She took him by the hand, slipped quietly out the back door, and disappeared. We sat and stared at the huge grandfather clock as its hands clicked through time. At fifteen-minute intervals the cuckoo bird crowed. We were silent. Thirty minutes after Nathan, I left the house by myself, carefully following Mama's instructions to talk to no-one, keep my head down, and make my way directly to the train station. It was a long walk, but I knew the way, and I knew how important it was to get there safely.

We couldn't bring big suitcases because that would have attracted attention. So we each carried only a small satchel with a few clothes, photos, and personal items. Inge came next, only eight years old, but already having to make her way alone. Lastly, Mama left our house, slipping out the back door like a thief, jewels sewn into her clothes, abandoning the beautiful home she had tended for many years, the place where she had raised her children and that was to have been a refuge.

I was terrified that a stormtrooper would notice me, or Inge, little girls walking alone, or recognize Mama as the wife of a wanted fugitive, but miraculously no-one stopped us. Somehow we evaded attention, and we all met up at the Chemnitz train station. Mama bought tickets, and one by one we boarded the train bound for Amsterdam.

Germany was no longer safe. Once again the family was on the move. Eleven years after settling in Germany my mother was fleeing, this time with three young children. She left behind her friends, her siblings, her extended family, her community, almost all her belongings. She left her financial security, her husband's prospering business, her lovely home. She took her children and a few jewels sewn into the seams of dresses, and – in what was to become a pattern – fled quickly and without looking back. Our days of security were over. We were lucky to escape. Overnight we became refugees, fleeing blindly into another country where we didn't speak the language and had no home.

Two months after Hitler came to power, a few days after Papa's abrupt departure, and only hours after we had been raided, our entire family was en route out of Germany.

GENEK

LVOV, 1920S AND 1930S

Gimpel Bottner, known to friends and family as Genek, was raised in the city of Lvov, situated in the province of Galicia in western Ukraine. Galicia has changed allegiances many times over the years; though part of Poland when Genek was a boy, the area was at times controlled by Ukraine, at times by Austria-Hungary, and at other times by Russia.

During Genek's childhood, ethnic tensions exploded in Lvov, as Poles and Ukrainians fought for control of the city after World War One. In fact, even the city's name is contested and has changed over the years: Lvov to Poles, Lviv to Ukrainians, and Lemberg to Austrians and Germans.

It was in this tumultuous Galicia that Genek was born on April 1, 1911. Genek, despite a fiery temper, had a lively sense of humor: he always joked that he was a Galiciana first and foremost. He would inevitably accompany this announcement with a little sideways gesture of his hand, and a huge twinkle in his eye. Being a Galiciana meant he could be a bit of a thief, a bit of a rebel, and certainly one who would bend the law a little if it meant staying in the game. He said this half ironically. He didn't have the fondest memories of the place, but still, it was home. Being a Galiciana meant pulling a fast one when necessary.

Before World War Two Lvov boasted the third largest Jewish community in Poland, with over a hundred thousand Jewish inhabitants. One in three residents of Lvov was Jewish. There were many different sects of Jews in the city: Hassidim with their long black coats and curly sideburns, modern Reform Jews, and a Zionist community that longed for the formation of a modern Jewish state in Palestine. There were Jewish hospitals, a Jewish orphanage, Jewish theaters, Jewish sports clubs, and several Jewish newspapers. Genek's family was a fairly typical working-class one, consisting of tradesmen and small shop owners of the type who ran many of the businesses in Lvov.

Genek was the eldest of four boys. He lived with his father Ignacy (Yehudah) and mother Berta (Beila)(nee Fendrech), in the thriving Jewish quarter. Ignacy ran the family business, a small restaurant located at 121 Grodecka Street.

While certainly not Hassidic, his family was traditional, speaking Yiddish, sending the boys to cheder – Jewish school – and worshiping in one of the fifty working synagogues in the city. They observed Shabbos and the holidays, and had a large network of Jewish friends and extended family in the city and its environs. The family lived very modestly; money was always tight. When Genek was older he would help support them when he became a bookkeeper.

Genek's father, Yehudah, like Melly's father Leopold, had been conscripted to fight in the First World War for the Austrian-Hungarian army. Like Leopold, the experience left him traumatized and violent. When they were growing up he beat his four boys – Gimpel, Joseph, Moshe, and Ephraim – with a home-made whip. Moshe, called Mundek, the youngest and most

18

rebellious of the boys, was particularly singled out for punishment.

So life at home was rough, and despite its large Jewish population Ukraine was not an easy place to grow up a Jew. Antisemitism was rampant, and Genek's family lived in constant fear of pogroms. Every couple of years, especially in the spring around Easter time, throngs of thugs would take to the streets of Lvov, breaking into Jewish homes and stores, raping, killing, and rampaging. In 1917 and 1918 large-scale pogroms took the lives of over a hundred Jews in Lvov, injuring many more. As he grew older, Genek itched to fight back, but his mother begged him to avoid the violent streets.

Of average height but strong physique, Genek was a muscular young man with fair hair, his father's prominent nose and his mother's enormous blue eyes. Throughout his life he would enjoy robust physical health and have an aversion to illness or signs of weakness. He kept himself out of the street fights by playing football (soccer) in the Jewish sports clubs. Playing football would eventually open the door for him to get out of Galicia.

One of the few places where the divisions between ethnic groups faded a bit was in the world of sports. While Poles, Ukrainians, Russians, and Jews feared, loathed, and fought each other in the "regular" world, sports teams and the competition between them provided a place of relative detente. Still, while there were some "mixed" teams of different ethnicities, most were segregated into single ethnic groups.

The Jewish community had a successful presence in the sporting world in Lvov, especially during the interwar decades. Lvov Jews proudly boasted that one of their native sons had founded the Jewish sports league called Hesmonia, preceding the chapters later founded in Krakow and Warsaw, Lvov's "bigger sister" cities. The league's name was a Biblical reference to a group that fought for the Hebrew people's religious and political independence in ancient times. Lvov Hesmonia had teams playing twelve different sports. Genek played for the popular and successful Lvov football team.

Football was definitely the super-star sport in Lvov. In 1923, when Genek was twelve, Hesmonia opened the largest sports stadium in the city, able to hold ten thousand spectators, and to seat two thousand in seats. The Jewish populace was elated with this opening, even empowered enough to host international football matches at the stadium. In 1925 a landmark match between Polish and Ukrainian teams was played in this Jewish-owned stadium, helping to ease tensions between ethnic groups that had been feuding for years.

The Jewish teams were still sometimes the objects of antisemitism, however. There were accusations of unfair penalties levied against them by the Polish authorities. And in 1932, only nine years after its debut, tragically, the cherished stadium was destroyed by fire.

There were other important sporting leagues in the area; one was called Maccabi. The Maccabi movement began around the turn of the century in Central Europe, when Jewish athletes, eager to compete in the sporting world, experienced antisemitic exclusion. Many smaller clubs eventually merged to create the Maccabi World Movement, modeled after the Olympics, with international athletes competing in a different country each time the Games convened. The first international European Maccabi Games were held in Prague in 1929, moving the following year to Antwerp, Belgium.

There were many teams and many leagues, and there was a lot of complicated politics going on in the Galiciana world of football in the 1920s and '30s. Eventually some leagues merged and coalesced into the Polish Football Association.

Genek played for one of these teams, although whether it was Lvov Hesmonia, a Maccabi team, or another team is lost to history. In fact, it is possible that he belonged to more than one Lvov team during his youthful soccer years. What is known is that as a member of one of these soccer teams, Genek went to Belgium in the mid-1930s for an international competition. Most likely, then, he was playing for a team called Pogon, for that team did in fact compete in France and Belgium in the spring of 1934. That would have made Genek twenty-three when he first went abroad.

At any rate, somewhere between 1934 and 1936 Genek, a street-wise young man from a tough Polish town, had the opportunity to go to Belgium, a country so much more refined and cultured that he spoke for the rest of his life about the impact this eye-opening experience had on him.

He was dumbfounded by Belgium. His entire life he had lived in an old fashioned Orthodox Jewish community in a tumultuous and violent part of eastern Poland. Suddenly he saw that the world was a big place. There existed tree-lined boulevards with outdoor cafes and restaurants, where people sipped hot chocolate thick as honey and nibbled on delectable cream puffs. There were enormous plazas where flower markets erupted in riots of color, where pretty girls rode bicycles while chatting with their friends in singsong French. The Belgians wore beautiful clothes, the girls artfully coiffed and impossibly sophisticated, so different from the babushkas and other peasant garb the girls wore at home. And nobody seemed to notice, or to care, about one's nationality or religious affiliation. Mostly, people here seemed happy and prosperous in a way Genek cannot have dreamed possible, and there did not seem to be any threat of violence in the streets.

Struck by the tolerance and peace of the first country he had ever traveled to outside his homeland, Genek, for the very first time, must have realized that life could be lived in a safer, more harmonious setting.

One of his teammates, a friend and fellow Jew named Hiss, was even more smitten. Hiss did not want to return to Lvov; he wanted to stay on in Belgium, run off when the match was over, desert the team when the time came for their return. He talked to Genek of staying, of seeking out the Jewish community in Antwerp, perhaps, and making a new life for themselves. Of course, this would have been highly illegal. The young men had no papers, no visas, no right to stay on.

And Genek, though sorely tempted, had his family back home to think of. It would have felt impossible to not return home. His parents, his brothers, his cousins, his friends, his entire life was back there. Also he had a girlfriend. It was difficult in Lvov, unpleasant at times, but if he didn't return, not only would Yehudah and Beila grieve the loss of their firstborn, but they would lose the financial contributions he made to help them make ends meet. Genek was especially close to his mother Beila; the thought of leaving her back in Galicia would have been painful. And then there was the girl he hoped would marry him one day.

So the young men returned to Lvov with their team. But the idea of emigrating stayed with them. The two soccer players spent many long evenings together once home, talking endlessly, contemplating whether they would ever actually take the huge step of leaving.

Genek would have liked his family to come along. He spoke to his parents and brothers about the idea, but they demurred. Beila and Yehudah were simple hard-working folks who couldn't even imagine moving to a new country. Their whole life was here in Poland, their friends, their families, their synagogue. Genek's talk of moving to Belgium would have sounded like craziness. Besides, even if they wanted to, who could get papers to move? Jews were restricted from travel. His brothers, Joseph and Ephraim, ridiculed him. Only Mundek seemed intrigued. He was the toughest of the brothers, a street-smart scrabbler and frequently in trouble, and he didn't rule out leaving Lvov at some point, if the opportunity ever arose.

Genek's young woman was equally dismissive of the idea. A religious girl from a close-knit family, she declined Genek's proposal of leaving Lvov for a distant country. The idea of moving to a place with no family, where she didn't speak the language, didn't know the customs, must have been terrifying. She was fond of Genek, but if he wanted to marry her he would have to agree to staying in Lvov. That was home.

Despite his loved ones' dismissal, the idea of moving remained in Genek's mind, worrying him like a sore tooth. His friend Hiss continued trying to persuade him to leave with him. Genek had an agonizing choice to make. He can't have imagined a future for himself in Lvov, living in fear of the next pogrom. But if he left his family, he couldn't be sure that they would be alright. He couldn't know when would he see them again, or whether his girl would wait for him. On the other hand, he must have feared that if he didn't go, he would be squandering an incredible opportunity.

By now the year was 1936. Hitler had been Chancellor of Germany for three years, and trouble was brewing in Europe. Genek, a Jewish 25-year-old from Poland, knew there was no hope for him or Hiss to obtain the necessary documents for travel, never mind to legally work in Belgium. Yet slowly his resolve grew. Life was becoming more and more unstable; the Nazis in neighboring Germany were churning out increasingly horrific propaganda against the Jews. The Russians were on Poland's eastern border, likely gearing up for yet another invasion into Galicia. If they were going to leave, it seemed the time was now.

Genek studied the maps he had collected during his earlier journey. A thousand cold and dangerous miles across all of Poland and Germany stood between him and his goal of reaching Belgium. And Germany was really terrorizing, a hotbed of antisemitism, filled with increasingly virulent National Socialists. The Nazis hated Jews, hated communists; the stories of their brutality were terrible. The journey would be arduous and dangerous. But the time had come.

After a heart-wrenching goodbye to his family, and with tearful promises to be reconnected soon, Genek departed Lvov in the spring of 1936. Carrying a couple of days' provisions that Beila tucked into his rucksack, Genek, together with Hiss, started walking west. Although he did not know it at the time, Genek would never see Lvov, his girlfriend, his parents, or two of his brothers again.

They had scant ID. They had no means of legally crossing borders. If they were stopped and questioned they were doomed. They had very little money. But they were young and strong, athletic, and determined. They would travel together and look out for each other, and somehow make their way to a more enlightened country, find a way to start over, seize whatever opportunity life threw their way.

Because of their illegal status, the young men had to be cautious. Without documentation, they could not risk riding the trains. And so mostly they walked, sticking to back roads where they attracted little notice. Occasionally a farmer gave them a lift, driving them a few miles in a wagon or tractor, dropping them off a little closer to their goal. They slept in fields, taking turns standing guard to make sure they were not discovered by police or by soldiers, the other grabbing a few hours of shut-eye, then switching. Sometimes they were able to sneak into a barn, spending the night curled up in the straw beside the livestock, maybe stealing a few eggs before they made off in the pre-dawn hours to continue their trek west.

Maybe they were able to buy food at markets while they were still in Poland. They spoke the language, had the right currency. They may have begged farmers' wives for meals as they passed through, and perhaps they did well, two handsome young men, traveling by foot. When hungry enough, they probably helped themselves to produce from the fields they traversed. But once they crossed into Germany, they would have had to be extremely cautious, avoiding all contact with the locals. It was imperative to travel under the radar.

It's possible that they took a southern route, traveling part of the way through Czechoslovakia. It would make sense that they would try to minimize the time they spent walking through Nazi Germany.

It is hard to imagine walking a thousand miles without shelter or a reliable food source, withstanding rain and wind and mud, mosquitos, spiders, blisters, hunger, thirst, the beating sun, the chilly nights. Traveling on foot without a place to bathe or rest or wash their clothes. Traveling through hostile territory, fearing always an unexpected check point, a demand for documents they didn't possess. Taking turns staying awake while the other slept on the bare ground, trying to stay alert, on guard always for unexpected danger. Walking through homesickness, anxiety about their families, worry about what they were heading into. But they were young, and on the road, and that combination is pretty intoxicating. So maybe they had some good times too.

How long did the journey take? No-one really knows. If they walked an average of twenty miles a day the journey would have taken them fifty days. But it's probable that they really traveled farther than a thousand miles, as they had to skirt urban areas and check points. Even at this brisk pace, if in fact they were able to travel that fast, it's likely the journey took at least two months, and more likely three months.

Miraculously, they did eventually make it out of Germany and into the relative safety that was Belgium. They had walked across Poland, part of Czechoslovakia, and through Nazi Germany, and had made it out without being detained, without succumbing to exposure or hunger or disease. They had done it. They had no money, no visas, no passports. They did not speak French or Flemish. But they were out of Poland, and out of Germany, and they were ready for the next leg of their adventure.

Genek and Hiss had heard that there was a large Jewish population in the northern Belgian city of Antwerp, and so that is where they went. Genek must have cut a sorry figure after the arduous trek from Lvov. But he asked for help getting himself situated, and, as was the way in the Jewish Diaspora, received it. Now that he was in Antwerp it was time to figure out a new life for himself.

Genek had trained as a bookkeeper in Lvov, but there were no jobs for him in that field in Antwerp. The Jewish community here was involved in two thriving businesses: diamonds and furs. Genek realized he would have to learn a new trade. And so he apprenticed himself to a man he met, a furrier, learning the trade that would be his from then on. He learned how to cut and sew together inexpensive fur scraps, assembling gloves, hats, jackets, vests, and muffs. Eventually he established a little atelier in his apartment, a corner devoted to his trade, where he created his wares. These items he then sold, either to a middle-man or, when possible, directly to the locals of Antwerp.

So he made ends meet by sewing furs, even sending a little money home to his folks in Galicia when he could. But he must have missed his family, his community. Genek was lonely. He realized pining for his girlfriend back home was not getting him anywhere. She had elected to stay in Lvov. She would not be joining him in Antwerp. It's clear that he must have been feeling like this, because by 1938 Genek had started thinking about getting himself a wife.

MELLY

AMSTERDAM AND ANTWERP

When we got to Amsterdam we were homeless. Gone were the servants and the luxurious home. We had escaped the Nazis, but we no longer had a place to even lay our heads. There was literally nowhere for our family to go. We got off the train and wandered the damp city streets, trying to locate Papa and figure out what to do next.

To my great dismay, Mama told us children that we would be going to an orphanage. There was nowhere else for us to sleep in Amsterdam. It was temporary, she told us, just until she and Papa could find a place for us to live. Resolutely she marched us into a dreary institution in this foreign city, conversed with the matron and then gave us stern instructions to behave.

This was the first time our new reality really hit me. I was so angry. So incredibly bitter that Hitler had robbed me of my life, of my home. I was bereft as Mama walked out of that orphanage, leaving Inge and Nathan holding hands at the door, crying. I thought Mama was abandoning us forever. Furiously, I kicked at the doorframe, impotent with rage. Take care of your brother and sister, Melly, were Mama's last words to me as she left.

The days passed in a cold and lonely blur but, true to her word, Mama did come back for us within a couple of weeks. Papa had found us a house to rent in the village of Scheveningen, on the Dutch coast. We collected our few meager belongings, stuffed them back into our satchels, and eagerly left that awful orphanage, excited again as we boarded the train for our new home.

Slowly we began making our life over in Scheveningen. The cottage we lived in was small but cozy. Mama enrolled Inge and me in school. At eleven I found myself in a Dutch classroom, where I only understood a few words that were being said. But I learned the language quickly.

Papa, who was becoming ever stranger, developed an obsession with swimming. The beach was very close to the house. Every morning he woke up little Nathan before dawn, and the two of them waded into the frigid waters of the North Atlantic just a few hundred yards from our cottage, swimming for about an hour in the choppy seas. I was happy to be excluded from this daily dunking, gratefully snatching a few extra minutes in my warm bed. But little Inge felt left out. I often heard her crying after Papa and Nathan left the cottage, heartbroken that she was not invited to join them.

Instead of feeling sorry for Inge, I was irked by her pitiful whining. Grow up, I told her, you are such a little baby. No wonder Papa doesn't take you swimming. Inge would cry even harder when I said that. It was during our time in that cottage that poor Inge tried to hang herself. Like I said, I was cruel to my sister. Good God, thinking about that is terrible.

Now, Nathan, the family darling, was considered a child prodigy. Papa had started teaching him to read Hebrew while we were still in Chemnitz, lifting the burden of Torah study off my shoulders and transferring it squarely onto my little brother's. But, unlike my reluctant compliance, Nathan took to learning like a fish to water, memorizing tracts of Torah and making my dour father beam with pride.

Papa and Nathan could usually be found with their heads together at the kitchen table in our cottage by the sea, reading and discussing Talmud, while we girls tiptoed around them, trying not to disturb. My brother was all of five years old when we arrived, his feet didn't even touch the floor as he sat at the table, but he was already well on his way to being prepared for his Bar Mitzvah, or so it seemed to me at any rate. Inge and I helped Mama prepare the meals, wash the clothes, and tidy the cottage while Papa and Nathan studied.

Papa became convinced that Nathan was a genius, a scholar who needed a great teacher, a rebbe, to further his education. He began making inquiries. Clearly the European continent was rife with prospects, but eventually Papa decided that Nathan's best chance for study was in London. An added bonus was that Papa had some business contacts there; also it was further from the Nazis.

And though we were safe and living a pretty normal life in Holland, we were conscious, of course, of the terror that Hitler was promulgating back in Germany. Stories of anti-Jewish legislation and repression percolated across the border. We listened to the radio, we read the papers, we heard the gossip. So while we felt incredibly lucky to be out, we worried about family and friends who were left behind. When Mama lit the Shabbos candles on Friday nights she always said a special prayer for her family still back in Germany.

Eventually, maybe a year or so after our arrival in Scheveningen, Papa and Nathan departed for London, leaving my mother, me, and Inge behind. They stayed in London for about a year. My brother studied with a rebbe, and learned English too, according to the letters we received from them. Papa tried to make contacts for his glove and sock manufacturing business while Nathan went to school. I missed Nathan, but overall this was a nice quiet time for Mama and us girls, with less drama than when Papa was home.

I continued attending school in Scheveningen, as did Inge. We were both very good students. Inge won some kind of math prize which made her incredibly proud. Of course, we were only girls, and the message we received was that it didn't really matter that much whether we succeeded at school. Our mother was vaguely pleased for Inge, but only Nathan was the prodigy, only a son's learning would be cause for celebration. I filed away this slight, as I had so many others, bringing them out to review in my mind's eye late at night as I lay on my bed trying to get to sleep.

Eventually Papa and Nathan returned. I don't know exactly why; I suppose they couldn't be estranged from the family forever. When they got back – it must have been 1936 by then – the family moved to Antwerp, Belgium. There was not much work for my father upon his return to Holland, and Antwerp had a larger Jewish community and more business prospects. Papa was still trying to make a go of business ventures in those years, although his behavior was becoming more erratic and bizarre. His obsession with religion continued, escalating as the years went on.

Once again I had to leave behind the friends I had made, leave Holland, which had become familiar, and enroll in a new school in a new city, a new country. In Antwerp they spoke Flemish, which thankfully was similar enough to Dutch that I was able to get by. I was fourteen by this time, surly and self-absorbed, resentful of another move, resentful of my family. I spent a lot of time in my own head, imagining a bright future away from the chaos that had become my life, fantasizing about a handsome man who would be struck by my beauty and sweep me away. I stayed in school, it was easy enough to get good grades, but my mind was far away.

Mostly what I recall about those years is that Papa was losing his grip on reality. Increasingly paranoid, he made us keep the curtains drawn in case people were snooping on us. He went on long raves about the Messiah coming, sometimes seeming to think that he was the Messiah. Mama became quiet and drawn, worried not only about her husband's mental health but about making ends meet and supporting her three growing children.

One day when I came home from school she told me that she was going to start working. This was a shock. Mama had been such a lady in Chemnitz, supervising her servants and making sure her household ran like clockwork. I couldn't imagine her working outside the home. But needs must.

There was a kosher patisserie, Mama told me, called Jalonjinsky's. Mr. Jalonjinsky, the Jewish owner, baked his goods at his primary location in downtown Antwerp, but he wanted to expand. Mama was going to run a secondary location located at Kleine Beerstraat 1, on the corner with Van Ruusbroecstraat. I knew the corner she meant; it was right in the Jewish quarter of the city. Mama said she needed my help. Someone had to pick up the pastries at the downtown bakery and bring them to "our" patisserie, and that someone was going to be me. You can use your bicycle to transport the baked goods, Mama told me. You'll have to go early in the morning, before school.

There was more. Papa was going to go to a hospital that cared for people with mental illness. It was unthinkable for him to be admitted to a goyishe hospital. There were no Jewish mental hospitals in Belgium, she said. The only Jewish asylum was back in Holland, in a town called Apeldoorn, so that was where he would be going for a while. Who knew, God willing, maybe he would get better, and be able to eventually come back home.

So that is what happened. Papa went to Apeldoornse Bos, a very large and well-respected Jewish mental hospital back in Holland. We went to visit him a couple of times in the ensuing years, and I remember an enormous country estate tucked into expansive woods, with vast well-manicured lawns and beautiful gardens. The hospital looked like a fancy museum from the outside. I am pretty sure the inside was not quite so elegant but, like I said, this was a highly respected institution staffed by the best Jewish psychiatrists in Europe, along with scores of lovely Jewish nurses. Papa always seemed to be well cared-for when we visited. It was so big, it almost seemed like its own little city. In 1938, the capacity of the hospital peaked at 900 patients! With all the staff, there were well over a thousand people there. Tragically, Papa never did get better. He stayed at the hospital until 1943, when the Nazis came in and brutally evacuated the entire place, and loaded everyone onto trucks bound for Auschwitz. Not just the patients, but those lovely nurses too. But once again, I am getting ahead of myself.

It was 1937 when Papa left Antwerp for the hospital, and Mama started running the patisserie on Kleine Beerstraat. There was a tiny apartment above the bakery, and Mama and we children moved in there. I hated it. Inge and I had to share a bed, and we fought a lot. There was no privacy. I was a moody teenager who craved personal space. It was not an easy time for me, nor for my family who had to live with my dark moods.

Every morning before school I cycled to Jalonjinsky's, picking up trays of warm croissants, sticky buns, cinnamon sticks, and whatever delectables had been baked that morning. If the weather was fine I actually enjoyed this early morning errand. I would help myself to a pastry, load the trays onto the back of my bike, and then cycle over to "our" patisserie where Mama was waiting to open up for the day. The scent of freshly baked sweets wafted through the air as I biked the Antwerp streets. I loved the feeling of being young, free, and on the move, the wind blowing through my hair. On cold rainy days, I did not have such a nice time, but I had to do the pick-up just the same. After school I came back to help Mama wait on customers and to clean up before we closed for the evening.

Soon the job of running the bakery by herself got to be too much for Mama. She suggested that I drop out of school – I was sixteen by then – and start working with her full-time in the shop. She couldn't afford to hire anyone else, and so I was the obvious solution. Inge was helping too, of course, but she was too young to drop out of school. I was terribly resentful. Why did I always have to be the one who worked? Why couldn't I have a normal adolescence, go to school, flirt with boys? I didn't really care about my studies that much, but I didn't want to be cooped up behind a counter waiting on customers all day. I wanted to have fun. With Papa out of the house I felt freer to voice these objections. Mama and I started to argue in earnest.

Well, I eventually did as Mama asked, but I managed to eke out a little something for myself too. Soon after I began working full-time in the patisserie, I found out that a room was available to let in the apartment building across the street. The manager, a customer of ours, said I could stay there for a ridiculously cheap rent. Mama, exhausted I think by my moodiness, agreed to let me move in there. It gave her and the younger kids a little more elbow room in the cramped apartment above the patisserie. We didn't think about the manager's motives.

At first I loved having my own place, even if it was a mere shoebox of an apartment. After my long days of cycling to pick up pastries, then waiting on customers, sweeping, wiping, and organizing, I loved having a quiet private retreat to go home to. It was a luxury to stretch out my long legs in my own bed without my little sister there to annoy me. I always did like my privacy. Unfortunately, it didn't last long.

Like most young girls, I continued to idly fantasize about romance. I had grown tall and shapely, and I couldn't help but notice the glances men gave me on the street as I cycled by. It was all so new, scary, but also intoxicating to realize I was desirable. Would a handsome prince arrive at my doorstep one day to sweep me off my feet? I was incredibly naive and inexperienced. In pre-war Europe, Jewish girls from a traditional family were practically cloistered; we did not get the chance to date or even have friendships with boys. But it was fun to daydream.

And dreamland was my only happy place. By 1938, further bad news was coming out of Germany. In November we heard about Kristallnacht, a night of violence against Jews that resulted in burned synagogues, including the beautiful old shul I had loved in Chemnitz. Jewish businesses had had their store windows smashed, their wares looted, and Jewish men and women had been beaten and killed by thugs in the streets throughout the country. Thousands of Jewish men were arrested, most sent to concentration camps. How was this possible? What was happening to our friends and relatives? I retreated further into my private world, my body going through the motions in the patisserie, but my mind a million miles away.

So yes, I had some girlish dreams about men, but the only people beside my family that I interacted with were the customers who came into the patisserie. Our customers were all Jewish, this being a kosher bakery after all, and most were immigrants. A majority of the Jews in Belgium at that time were refugees who had left their homes in Eastern Europe, fleeing persecution. The Jewish community in Antwerp had mushroomed as war loomed. Of course, many of our customers were female, and most of the men who came in had a female companion on their arm. Also, they almost all spoke Yiddish, which reeked of ignorant shtetl life to my ears. I always responded in German – I could understand Yiddish but couldn't speak it, and frankly had no desire to. There were some men who came in alone; maybe they were single – sometimes a man would try to flirt with me. To me, though, these were strangers with backward accents, and I ignored them. I was in that twilight period between girlhood and womanhood, intrigued by the idea of men more than by the actual ones I met.

So I worked in the patisserie during the day, but went back to my own place across the street once we closed. One night while I was fast asleep in my tiny flat, my door opened. The sound woke me, and I sat up with a small scream. The building manager, the man who had "generously" rented me the apartment, was standing in my doorway. I could smell the schnapps on his breath. My heart started pounding. What are you doing here? I cried. He started walking toward my bed, looking at me in a way I instinctively knew was dangerous.

I grabbed my pillow and held it tightly against my nightgown, trying to shield myself from this near-stranger who had invaded my room. My whole body started shaking. The man lunged at me. Screaming at the top of my lungs now, I kicked him in the stomach, my foot landing hard in his soft gut. He lurched away drunkenly, cursing, and I flew out of the room, down the stairs, out the front door, and across the street to Mama's apartment. Pounding on the door, I woke the entire family, and kept them up for the rest of the night with my hysterical recounting of what had occurred. Mama was aghast. Melly, Melly, she kept saying, oy va voy, Melly. What will be the end of all this, Melly? Needless to say I moved back into the tiny family apartment that night and resumed my resentful bed-share with Inge.

Looking back, I feel sorry for my mama. Her formerly comfortable life had evaporated. Her husband had gone mad and been shipped off to an institution, leaving her responsible for three children in a strange country. Her eldest daughter was resentful and moody, becoming ever more unruly without a father, wanting independence that was obviously unsuitable, and was already getting into trouble – imagine if that man had violated me! How was she to keep me safe?

At the time, though, I had no insight into anyone else's troubles, consumed as I was – as I guess all teenagers are – with my own unhappiness. I was aware of what was going on in the world, that is

35

true. We all were very aware of the rising power of the Nazis in Germany. But that was so dreadful that I pushed it out of my mind whenever possible. That kind of problem was too overwhelming. No, my worries were more mundane. I brooded about my loss of a nice home, my lack of privacy, my annoying sister, my desire to break away from the family and lead a glamorous life.

But I guess Mama was more distraught than I realized. And conversations were apparently going on, plans being made, that I knew nothing about. You see, that has been the story of my life.

Shortly after that awful incident with the apartment manager, and I will never forget this day as long as I live – I was seventeen years old – Mama announced that we would be having a wedding soon.

A wedding.

She was very matter of fact about it. I was in the process of emptying out the pastry racks, wiping off the crumbs that had accumulated on the bottom shelves. I was only half listening to her.

Oh, who is getting married? I responded.

You are.

A WEDDING
BELGIUM 1938

Genek had been in Antwerp for a couple of years when he first saw the beautiful brunette on her bicycle. She was young, with long legs, creamy skin, and a dreamy look on her face. Something about her must have caught Genek's fancy. He soon found himself going down to the street early in the morning when he knew she would be riding by, timing it so he could catch a glimpse of the girl on the bicycle loaded with pastries. One day he followed her, and found that she took the baked goods to a kosher patisserie run by her mother. Genek quickly became a frequent customer at the patisserie. The mother, Gertrude, must have reminded him of some of his aunts back in Poland, and the pastries temporarily assuaged his endless hunger. He learned that the girl's name was Melly.

He was in his mid–twenties by now, and Genek wanted a woman. He thought it was time he got a wife. He tried to flirt with the girl, but she seemed to look right though him, barely answering when he spoke to her. Under normal circumstances he might have hired a matchmaker, or had his father approach the girl's father to discuss a possible match. But these were not normal times. He was alone in

Belgium. And the girl's father was away too, apparently. So Genek approached the mother.

Gertrude rebuffed him. No, Melly was too young to be married, she told him, and her husband wasn't there to make a match anyway. Her answer made him want the girl even more. Genek persisted. He told Gertrude he would be a good provider. His fur business was thriving. Wouldn't the family want the young girl settled with a nice Jewish husband? Where was Mr. Offner? Could Genek appeal to him, perhaps?

Eventually Gertrude explained that her husband was up in Holland, confined to a hospital, so there really was no point in discussing Melly at this time. Undaunted, Genek decided he would go up to Apeldoorn to make his case directly to Melly's father. He took the train north, and met with Leopold in the fall of 1937, the two men sitting on a bench on the beautiful hospital grounds. Genek asked Leopold for Melly's hand in marriage.

But Leopold was not impressed with Genek. The man was a coarse Polack who did not speak German. Worse, he was barely knowledgeable in Jewish law. No, this furrier was not the man he had in mind for Melly. His daughter would wed an ultra-Orthodox man like himself, a rabbi maybe. Leopold had retreated further into his religious delusions by now; his entire life was consumed with religiosity. He told Genek no.

So Genek returned to Antwerp without the answer he wanted, but determined nonetheless to win the beautiful girl's hand. He continued frequenting the patisserie, chatting up the mother, and trying to catch the girl's eye. Melly persisted with her aloof indifference. Genek's ardor mounted.

And then one day in February, a miracle. Gertrude pulled him into a corner of the bakery and asked if he was still serious about Melly. Barely believing his ears, Genek assured her he was, most definitely. He had only the most honorable of intentions. He wanted to marry the girl. As soon as possible.

Too happy to ask questions, Genek must have been curious, nonetheless, about what had made the mother change her mind. But better not to look a gift horse in the mouth, he decided. The girl was ripe and beautiful, and soon she would be his.

Gertrude had seized on the only plan she could think of to keep her rebellious daughter safe. Did she have reservations about marrying her eldest off to a man the girl barely knew, and obviously cared nothing for? Undoubtedly. But better a suboptimal marriage to a Jewish man who wanted her and would keep her safe than a difficult teen running wild, bringing shame onto the entire family. She herself had married a man her parents had picked; it had not been perfect, but she had survived. Melly would too.

So I will tell Melly, Gertrude continued to Genek. It is settled.

And so Melly was informed. There would be a wedding soon. Whose? Yours.

She was just seventeen years old. There would be no further discussion on the subject.

Four months later, on June 30, 1939, Genek and Melly stood under the chuppah in Antwerp and were pronounced man and wife by the rabbi. Invitations had gone out, and those who could attend the wedding were there. Genek's family was not in attendance; they were all back in Galicia. Some of Gertrude's brothers and sisters had made it out of Germany, and they were at the wedding – Uncle Herman with his wife and young son; Tante Sarah too. It is unclear whether Melly's father Leopold ever consented to the marriage; at any rate, still hospitalized in Holland, he did not attend the wedding. Young Nathan had a great time – skipping from table to table, snatching and downing glass after glass of abandoned champagne, eventually falling asleep under one of the tablecloths. Inge watched quietly, as was her way.

Genek peered at his beautiful bride, breathlessly anticipating the moment when he could finally be alone with her. Melly, her face a study in despair, refused to smile as the photographer snapped away. Her wedding pictures show the most unhappy bride.

MELLY
MARRIED LIFE

What can I tell you? I was married at seventeen to a peasant, a brute. The man had no class. He didn't know the difference between good food and bad – he ate anything! My new husband was always hungry, and I hated seeing the way he shoveled everything into his mouth. He could make a chicken disappear in two minutes. He even ate the neck, bones and all. And he put jam on his herring, can you imagine? When I tried to dispose of kitchen scraps he stopped me. He would rather eat old food than let me get rid of it. It's better to throw in than to throw out, he would cackle, patting his belly. Oh, he loved that joke. He thought he was clever. Another favorite joke – Melly, if you eat garlic every day for a hundred years, you will live a long time! Oh my God, if I had a penny for every time I heard those two jokes, I'd be a wealthy woman, believe me.

The man was strong as an ox; he didn't believe in getting sick. Once, I remember, his back hurt. Instead of resting, Genek threw himself down the stairs. Seriously. That was his way of dealing with discomfort.

He was all about the body – his physical strength, his ravenous appetite, his impatience with weakness. I was a creature of the mind. I felt very alone with Genek. He spoke to me in Yiddish. I answered tersely in German. We had so little in common: not even a language.

And he was on me constantly. In those days women were expected to submit to their husband's sexual advances. A woman's desires were not considered. I tried to escape him, but we lived in such cramped quarters, it was useless. Within a month I was pregnant. My girlhood, such as it was, was really over.

Genek had no patience with the fatigue and nausea I experienced early in the pregnancy. He didn't believe in weakness – he wanted me to snap out of it. As if I wanted to feel sick and tired! We had some terrible fights. When he wasn't home I allowed myself to cry, but in front of him I kept up a stony front. I would not allow him to think I was soft and hurting. I cleaned, I shopped, I cooked, I pretended I felt well, and I tried my best to avoid him. But of course that was impossible.

We had moved into our own small apartment. Genek continued with his fur business, creating a small atelier in one room of our flat. He expected me to help with sewing and such. I did it, but I hated it, hated everything about it, the dead animal pelts, the smell, the nastiness of the entire business. But what could I do? We needed the money, we had to pay rent, buy food. My husband was a furrier; I became his assistant.

One thing I will give him credit for: Genek was thrilled about my pregnancy. To be honest, I was not. I was appalled to be pregnant at seventeen. But Genek wanted a son so badly. He went around whistling and muttering endearments to the unborn child, calling him bubbeleh, having imaginary conversations with the baby. And eventually, though it took a few months, I too started thinking of the swelling in my belly as an actual baby. I was full of wonder as my middle expanded, as my breasts grew, and as I felt the first flutter of kicks in my womb.

But what a time to be bringing a child into the world. Hitler had already invaded Poland and Czechoslovakia. The Nazis clearly wanted to control all of Europe, and they were viciously and virulently antisemitic. We heard bone-chilling stories about atrocities happening to Jews in Poland. Genek was distraught with worry about his family. I felt for him about this, I really did. For the moment we were safe, but would that safety last? Would Belgium remain a sanctuary for us? As my pregnancy advanced the stories got worse. I concentrated on my unborn child, and prayed that he would be healthy.

On April 23, 1940, I gave birth. My son was a big baby, and the delivery was very difficult. But he was so beautiful. I fell in love completely and forever. Feeling his little hand curl around my finger, gazing into his wide eyes, smelling his scalp, and feeling him nuzzle into my body elicited feelings of such magnitude that they rocked me to my core. I felt fierce. This child was mine and I would do anything to protect him. On that day I ceased being a moody teenager and became a mother. Never again would my needs come first; now my darling son was all that mattered.

Genek was as ecstatic as me. He too adored the bubbeleh. We named the baby Alfred Izzak, but we called him Bobby, the bubbeleh we had been waiting for, and he brought us both such immense joy. Genek and I did not see eye to eye on many things. But about our son we agreed wholeheartedly: he was beautiful, precious, the best thing either of us had ever created.

Our joy was short-lived. Just three weeks after Bobby's birth, on May 10, 1940, Hitler invaded Belgium. The Belgian army was completely overpowered; they didn't stand a chance against the German forces. Within weeks Belgium surrendered to the Germans, and Nazi tanks rolled into the streets of Antwerp. Much of the Belgian government fled to England, where they established a government in exile. King Leopold and Queen Elizabeth, the sovereigns, remained in Belgium but were essentially powerless. Belgium was under occupation.

Once again I heard the terrifying sound of Nazi boots marching past my window. I was eighteen years old, recovering from childbirth, married to a virtual stranger, and again living in the shadow of terror. Only now I had a newborn baby to protect.

The arrival of the Nazis sparked complete pandemonium. All we could think about, like everyone around us, was how to escape. The streets were thronged with panicked Belgians trying to flee the country. By foot, by car, by horse, by wagon, by train – any way possible – everyone wanted to get to France, still free, or even better to England.

The Jewish population was especially panicked. Most of the Jews in Antwerp at that time were not native Belgians; like us, most had fled Germany and Eastern Europe ahead of Hitler. Having the Germans invade Belgium was the most terrifying thing imaginable. The Nazi invasion of our adopted country brought home the realization that we were no longer safe. The enemy was here. Once again we had to run.

Our family – my mother and siblings, Genek, me, and little Bobby – joined the throngs streaming toward the train station. People were carrying suitcases and bundles, bags of food, children. Everyone was pushing, trying to get ahead, hoping to flee to safety. It was obvious that there wouldn't be enough trains to carry all these people. I clutched Bobby to my chest and followed Genek's back as he plowed through the crowded streets and into the melee that was the train station.

Somehow we managed to board a train heading for the city of Ostend, Belgium's port on the North Sea. Our hope was to catch a ship from there to England. Like everyone else, we were desperate to get out of Belgium, and if we could put the English Channel between us and the Nazi invaders, so much the better. The train was terribly crowded. The five of us and the baby squeezed into a tiny compartment, little Bobby suspended in a sling between two poles, swaying as the train chugged slowly out of Antwerp.

What do I remember about that train ride? It seemed we were stopped more than we were moving. I think we could have made better time if we had been walking, though I was grateful we were not. Every few minutes the brakes came on. Every time the train stopped there was a collective groan. I remember the crush of humanity, the heat of all those bodies crowded together, the fear. I swear I could smell the fear. And the planes. German planes descended out of the sky without warning, buzzing down like crazed hornets, dropping bombs onto the Belgian countryside. I watched the plumes of smoke rise into the spring air. So this was war. I expected a bomb to hit our train any minute.

We were on that train, stopping and going, for maybe two days. Ostend is only about seventy miles west of Antwerp, so you see how slowly we were moving. We had a little food, not much. During longer stops Nathan hopped down and ran around trying to buy some provisions, and to find some milk for Bobby. My milk supply was already dwindling, and I was in anguish when the baby cried with hunger. Of course there wasn't much food to buy: everyone was panicking, hoarding and hiding what they had. But Nathan was resourceful: he managed to get some milk for the baby, and some bread and cheese for the rest of us.

Needless to say, we didn't get to Ostend in time to catch that ship. By the time we arrived it had left port. There would be no escaping to England for us. Instead we joined the desperate masses trying to get to France. We got on another train heading for the French city of Lille, about sixty miles south of Ostend. Again we endured overcrowding and hunger, worrying about whether the French would allow us in, or whether we would be turned back at the border. Again I suspended little Bobby in his sling, watching anxiously as he swayed to and fro, praying I would have enough milk to feed him.

There was such chaos everywhere, everyone trying to get out of Belgium. You can't imagine the stream of refugees we were part of. We were lucky to be on a train; I saw so many people walking toward the French border as we went by, so many desperate families on foot. And the Germans kept bombing them. When people saw the planes approach they threw themselves into ditches or sprinted for the woods. The lucky ones picked themselves back up after the planes departed; the bodies of the unlucky ones lay in the dusty roads.

How could my child have been born into such a nightmare? Little did I know, but much worse was yet to come.

GERMAN OCCUPATION
BELGIUM 1940-1941

In the first weeks after the Germans took power in Belgium, tens of thousands of local people, Jews and non-Jews, flocked north to the coast, or west toward the French border. They were trying to escape the German occupation, hoping to either cross into France, which was still free, or else get on a boat for England. Roads were jammed with refugees traveling in every manner imaginable – by foot, by bicycle, by horse-drawn cart, and occasionally by car – as they streamed away from the major urban areas. Families carrying small children and bundles of their most important possessions trudged toward towns like Lille, on the French border. Thousands of terrified refugees clogged the roads, only to be turned away, denied access into France. The refugees had no choice but to turn back and head home. All the while, German planes flew low, dropping bombs on the fleeing civilians, increasing their terror and adding to the mayhem.

At this point, however, the German soldiers were civil to the locals. They were under instruction to win the local populace over. So young blond German soldiers smilingly told the Belgians to turn around and head home, not to worry. And the Belgians were reassured. Maybe the Nazi occupation wouldn't be too bad. Sure, the planes were shooting at them, but this was war, and they were on the run. Maybe it would be better to just go home, sit tight and hope for the best.

Melly, Genek, Bobby, Gertrude, Inge, and Nathan were among the hordes trying to escape Belgium as the Nazis arrived in the spring of 1940. They made it to the French border, but no further. German soldiers stopped them as they tried to cross into France and asked them to return to their home in Antwerp. Although they were rebuffed, there was no trace of the violence or antisemitic hostility the family had expected and feared. The German soldiers were polite, affable, even friendly.

Since the trains were so overcrowded, the majority of the would-be refugees had no way to return to their homes. Many had to walk back the way they had come. But a group of German soldiers took pity on the Offner-Bottner clan, traveling as they were with a newborn baby; they offered them a lift back to Antwerp in the back of a German truck.

And so the family returned to Antwerp: Gertrude and her two younger children to their flat above the patisserie, and Melly, Genek, and Bobby to their own flat a few blocks away. They resumed the life they had led before the German occupation, running the patisserie and making fur vests and jackets. Everyone hoped the war would be over soon.

For the Germans, the first order of business was to recruit the support of the local people. So no overt hostilities were instituted in the first few months of occupation. The Nazis had an agenda, of course. But they bided their time, lulling the occupied nation into a false sense of safety before slowly beginning the persecution of the Jews.

Slowly but steadily, over the first eighteen months after taking power, the Nazis instituted their anti-Jewish measures through a series of ordinances. The plan was undertaken in a chillingly orderly, well thought-out, and systematic way.

Within months, the anti-Jewish "ordinances" – legal decrees – began. The Nazis first decreed that kosher butchering was illegal, making it very difficult for Jews to eat meat. Other anti-Jewish laws quickly followed, progressively limiting Jews' rights. It became illegal for Jews to own radios, to own real estate. Next, any business run by Jewish people was required to display a large sign in its window stating "Jewish Enterprise." Jews' ID cards were next altered, displaying a red stamp saying "JEW." After that, Jews were forbidden from owning businesses at all, and were banned from working as teachers, lawyers, doctors, or civil servants. Eventually Jewish children were not allowed to attend school.

How did the Nazis know who was Jewish?

The Germans manipulated leaders of the Jewish community into helping them. This is one of the most sinister aspects of Nazi rule, and one they employed effectively throughout the war in all occupied countries. Using both carrots and sticks, and as many falsehoods as it took, the occupiers convinced the Jewish leadership that cooperating with the Nazis would protect their community. The Jewish leaders, hoping to mollify the invaders and to avoid bloodshed, complied.

In Belgium, the Nazis ordered the Chief Rabbi, Salomon Ullmann, to form the Association des Juifs de Belgique (AJB). The Nazis appointed other Jewish leaders to be the directors of this agency, many against their will. The AJB became a puppet organization, with the Nazi leadership pulling the strings. The Jewish community, seeing that their most trusted leaders were heading this agency, dutifully cooperated with it.

As soon as it was formed, the Germans ordered the AJB to create a register of all Jews living in Belgium. The Nazis told the AJB that the purpose of this register was "to care for the social and legal needs of the Jewish population." By complying, the Jewish community inadvertently provided the Nazis with a careful list of Jewish families' names and addresses. Of course, this register would eventually be used as a ready-made guide to where Jews lived, who was in their household, etc. Because they succeeded in duping the AJB, the Germans had a handy road map when the time eventually came to find and round up Jews for deportation.

Belgium is composed of two different cultures: the Flemish north and the French south. Antwerp is in the Flemish area and Brussels in the French. Belgium is a tiny country, however, and the two cultures are interwoven and never more than a few miles from each other.

The predominantly Flemish city of Antwerp was home to a thriving Jewish population. Well over fifty thousand Jews lived in Antwerp at the dawn of the war, many of them non-Belgian Jews who had emigrated ahead of the Nazi occupation. The city had one of the most vibrant Jewish communities in Western Europe. Five synagogues, scores of Jewish schools, multiple Jewish professional organizations, sports clubs, and a thriving Yiddish theater, as well as several Yiddish newspapers, made the city a real center for Jewish culture. And the Jewish population was extremely involved in the diamond business, Antwerp's best-known industry. So Jews prospered in Antwerp in the 1930s and early 1940s.

Despite this, a culture of antisemitism was deeply rooted in Flemish tradition, and as the Nazi regime instituted anti-Jewish measures they received much more support from the Flemish population than from the French. On April 14, 1941, local pro-Nazi groups in Antwerp staged a pogrom, looting synagogues and burning Jewish businesses. In this city, the German agenda fell on fertile ground. The Germans may have instigated the riots, but the local populace carried out the violence. Antwerp would turn out to be a disaster for the Jewish community. In fact, of the fifty thousand

Jews inhabiting Antwerp at the start of the war, only eight hundred of those who stayed in the city would survive.

In the spring of 1941, in the wake of the "Antwerp Pogrom," as it became clear that the city was no longer safe for its Jewish inhabitants, many chose to move. Options were limited, but to many it seemed safer to relocate to Brussels, a larger city, predominantly French, and perhaps less antisemitic. In a bigger city where they were not known as Jewish, perhaps it would be easier to blend in.

And staying in Antwerp soon became impossible for Jews anyway. The local police succumbed to pressure from the German occupiers and issued all non-native residents with directives to leave the city. Both Genek and Melly received these orders.

The Offner-Bottner family was thus evicted from Antwerp. Gertrude abandoned the patisserie, which was almost impossible to run with the anti-Jewish measures in place anyway. Food supplies were dwindling, and Jalonjinsky was barely able to find the flour and butter to bake anymore. Genek and Melly packed up the atelier, gave up their apartment, took one-year-old Bobby, and moved to Brussels as well.

It was at this time, the spring of 1941, as it became obvious that anti-Jewish discrimination was increasing, that the family started trying to "pass" as non-Jewish. It helped that the names Offner and Bottner were German, and that they all – apart from Genek – spoke the language perfectly. It helped that they were newcomers in Brussels, where no-one knew them. And while they were obviously not native Belgians, it was safer to be perceived as German Christians than as Jews. Gertrude found a flat to rent in Brussels for herself, Inge, and Nathan. She enrolled the children in a secular school.

Genek and Melly found their own place on the top floor of a building on Rue Rogier, in the area of Brussels known as

Schaerbeek. The street was lined with three- and four-story buildings. Most apartments had a small balcony enclosed by a wrought-iron fence facing the street. They chose this neighborhood because it was not a "Jewish" one; most of their neighbors were non-Jews. One-year-old Bobby loved nothing better than to stand on the balcony looking down at people walking by. When his parents' back was turned he grabbed whatever item he could reach and threw it off the balcony, delighting in seeing it bounce off the sidewalk.

Once again Genek set up shop inside the apartment, stacking his fur scraps and hides on the shelves, and finding a nook for his sewing machine. He still had to work; they still had to sell the fur garments he made so they could earn a little money to buy food and pay rent.

In May 1941 an ordinance decreed that all Jewish males over sixteen years of age were responsible for compulsory labor duty. The Germans pressured the AJB into supplying ten thousand names, and these ten thousand young men received letters telling them to report for work duty on a certain date. The Jewish men were told to meet at the train station and that from there they would be transported to factories.

These ten thousand Jewish men and boys reported for "work duty" as ordered, and were transported into northern Belgium and northern France to do forced manual labor to aid the Nazi war machine. Some young men even reported voluntarily, hoping to appease the Germans with their obedience and willingness to cooperate. Once sent to the factories or work camps, however, they were literally worked to death. The unfortunate men who were conscripted were almost universally never heard from again.

It was never the Nazis' intention to have these young men return home. They were Jews, subhuman, useful only to do labor, and if they became too weak or sick to be useful, they were shipped to the death camps that were sprouting up in the wake of the Nazi "final solution." The boys' worried families wondered why they stopped receiving letters from their sons and brothers within weeks of leaving home.

In response to this work ordinance, Rabbi Ullmann sought help from the local authorities, and even reached out to Queen Elizabeth, the Queen Mother of King Leopold, the sovereign of Belgium. The queen allegedly called Hitler to plead on the Jews' behalf; he supposedly promised her that only foreign-born Jews would be deported on this work detail, and that Belgian Jews would be allowed to serve within the country. Apparently this promise placated the queen.

Since most of the Jews in Belgium were non-native this was a weak promise, and of course it was a lie; within a year the Nazis were rounding up and deporting Belgian-born Jews as well. Even the leaders of the AJB did not escape this fate. They, too, were arrested and deported in the second wave of raids.

It is important to note that of the roughly hundred thousand Jews residing in Belgium at this time, only about ten percent had Belgian citizenship. The rest were foreign Jews who had relocated to Belgium from other countries. It was, in fact, extremely difficult for immigrants to obtain Belgian citizenship. The laws did not even recognize children born in Belgium as citizens if their parents were foreign-born. So Bobby, for example, though born in Belgium, was not given Belgian citizenship at birth. The immigrants and their children were considered "stateless." This "stateless" status was yet another means the Nazi regime used to strip Jews of any rights, and to ensure that no government would protest their deportation and demise.

As the war progressed the Germans instituted stringent rations for the Belgian people. The rations were inadequate; everyone was hungry. By the winter of 1941 many were close to starvation. To obtain enough food to feed a growing child, Melly had to venture out, passing as a Christian German, to sell Genek's fur garments on the black market. Of course, this was highly illegal and dangerous. Anyone caught trading on the black market could expect arrest, deportation, even execution, if discovered by the Nazis. But with little choice, she proceeded, bartering to get milk, butter, flour, and vegetables to feed the family.

MELLY
LIFE UNDER OCCUPATION

It wasn't bad enough that we were living under Nazi tyranny and feeling squeezed by their ever-worsening decrees. It wasn't enough that I was desperately trying to get enough food to keep us alive, that I was risking my life every time I went out to barter on the black market, hoping the local police or the Nazi soldiers wouldn't decide to question me. It wasn't enough that I was terrified for Bobby's safety. No, in addition to all of that, I had my husband to contend with.

Genek wouldn't leave me alone. There was no birth control. I tried to put him off, asked him to be careful, to wait until a safer time of the month, to leave me alone, for God's sake – we had enough to worry about. But he wouldn't. Shortly after we arrived in Brussels I realized I was once again pregnant.

I think that was the first time I felt the blackness descend upon me. I had never been happy, my life had been hard, but when I discovered that I was pregnant in 1941 I took to my bed and could not get up. I curled up and wished I was dead. I could not have another baby now; the world was bleak and perilous. Every day was getting worse. What was I going to do? Genek yelled at me to get up. I closed my eyes and wept.

The only reason I was able to go on was Bobby. My beautiful son was my pride and joy. When he crept into my room and called, Mama!, I got out of bed. At age one he was walking, starting to talk, laughing and exploring, oblivious to the horrors around us. His blond curls and wide blue eyes made my heart sing.

For Bobby I would continue. I found out there was a Jewish doctor who would terminate a pregnancy. I guess I wasn't the only woman in desperate straits in wartime Brussels. I visited him in his clinic and asked for his help. He was sad, he told me. He used to bring life into this world; now all the Jewish patients came to him wanting to end the life inside them. I didn't want to hear his stories. I did what I had to do. It was painful, it was awful, it was terrifying. It was necessary. I went home and concentrated on keeping the child I had safe.

I would have liked to keep him indoors, away from the dangerous streets, but Bobby was obsessed with streetcars. From our balcony he could see them pass by, and all he wanted was to go on a car ride. Please Mama, please Papa, take me for a car ride! He was a child; he needed to go out sometimes. Thank God for Nathan – my younger brother loved my son, and after school he came to our apartment and took little Bobby out. Twelve years older than Bobby, he seemed somewhere between an uncle and a big brother to him. Down they went to the streetcar, riding it for hours, from one end of the line to the other, Bobby's eyes glued to the window, in heaven the entire time. As Bobby got a bit older, Nathan had to warn him not to talk. A child speaking Yiddish could attract unwanted attention. As Nathan came to collect him, my little son almost broke my heart by solemnly promising: Bobby nischt dreiden, Bobby won't talk.

I spent my days helping Genek sew his pelts, and whenever I could find yarn I fell back to my knitting hobby. Of course I made everything for Bobby – socks, hats, sweaters. We had nothing for him, so these woolens were a necessity. I will never forget the time that Bobby went out to the balcony, took off a sweater I had painstakingly knit him and threw it down onto the street! What can you do? He was a little child, he had no idea that yarn was precious. To him everything was a game.

Things were bad, and getting worse. The economy was a disaster. The Germans discontinued use of the Belgian franc, forcing the country to use Reichmarks. And when Germany went to war against Russia on the eastern front, the Germans demanded ever more of the Belgian foodstuffs for their army, and our rationing got even more stringent. We were allocated only 225 grams of bread per person, which provided less than 500 calories per day. Everyone had to stand in lines to collect bread, and in other lines to collect a little fat, half-spoiled potatoes or cabbage. Total rations were less than 1,000 calories. Everyone was hungry, everyone was too thin, and epidemics of disease were breaking out in the poorest neighborhoods.

I kept my eyes and ears open, always on the lookout for an opportunity. Sometimes I took the train out to the countryside, where there were still some groceries to buy. These trips were dangerous. Everything was dangerous. Buying food illegally was dangerous. Riding the streetcars was dangerous. I became quite the accomplished actress, throwing back my shoulders and striding "confidently" along the city streets to do my illegal errands. Because I knew this: showing fear was the most dangerous thing of all.

We were so cut off too. The Germans had confiscated all the Belgian media. We had no newspapers or radio to give us accurate reports of what was going on in the world. German news was dreck. They told us what they wanted us to hear; everyone knew that. Jews were not allowed to own radios, but we had ignored the mandate to turn ours over to the authorities. We kept our radio, and it was hidden at all times. Sometimes we were able to catch the BBC newscast from London. It was very scary to take out the radio and tune in to the BBC. This crime was punishable by death if we were caught. The news we did hear on the BBC did nothing to lift our spirits. One exception was when we learned that the United States had finally declared war on Germany and Japan after Pearl Harbor. That was reassuring. Maybe America could turn the tide of this war. But most of the news was terrible. We tried to be optimistic, but it was hard not to lose hope.

July 1942 brought even worse tidings. The Germans decreed that all Jews had to wear a yellow star on our clothes. The star had the word "Juif" printed on it, and failure to comply was grounds for execution. We were faced with a terrible dilemma: wear the star and be readily identified as Jewish, or ignore the mandate and risk execution if discovered. To add insult to injury, we had to pay for these stars! Yes, we were forced to use some of our precious money to buy this shameful symbol of our own persecution.

Sometimes we wore it, and sometimes we didn't. It depended on the situation. I often went out without the star, because I could easily pass as a non-Jew. Of course I didn't have paperwork to back that up, so it was an enormous risk. Genek looked Jewish, and had an accent, making it clear that he was foreign. And he had absolutely no documentation, so if he was stopped and questioned he would be arrested for sure. But Genek was outraged by the star ordinance, and usually refused to wear it. Of course, sometimes he had no choice. Mostly he stayed inside.

And again I got pregnant. And again I had an abortion. And again the blackness descended upon me and I took to my bed.

THE ANTI-JEWISH LAWS
BELGIUM, 1942

In July 1942 the Ordinance of the Yellow Star was passed – the decree that required all Jews aged six years and up to display a large yellow star with the word "Juif" on their garments. Failure to comply was grounds for execution. This ordinance was so blatant that many non-Jews, most thus far preoccupied with their own troubles, were outraged. The stars were such shocking talismans of the Jews' marginalization. The AJB, belatedly realizing they were being used to hurt their own people, refused to distribute the stars.

The non-Jewish populace differed in its reaction to the yellow star ordinance. In Antwerp, as noted, there was a widespread culture of antisemitism. In this Flemish city local authorities distributed the stars to the Jewish population and enforced the ordinance.

In Brussels, situated in the French part of the country, local authorities refused to cooperate, and the Germans had to distribute the stars themselves. In one instance of solidarity, the Cardinal of Brussels, Father Jozef-Ernest Van Roey, said in a sermon, "wearing of distinctive signs shames those who impose it and not those who wear it."

The end result was this: Jews were "branded" and ostracized more openly than ever before.

The French Belgians were among the most supportive in Europe when it came to helping the Jewish people during the war. The Flemish Belgians were much less inclined to help the Jews, and in next-door Holland the Dutch tended to support the Nazi anti-Jewish machine. The French in France, ironically, did not support the Jews for the most part; in that country the Germans easily tapped into the society's antisemitic base. Of course, there were outliers in every country, but these were the general trends. It is hard to make sense of these patterns, but the realization that the local peoples' attitudes could make such a huge difference in the outcome of the Nazis' plans is chilling, particularly as so few countries came to the Jews' aid.

Hitler and his henchman Eichmann were adept at assessing and manipulating the locals' attitude toward their Jewish neighbors. In countries like Poland and the Ukraine, where antisemitism was rampant, and violence entrenched, the Nazis handily whipped the masses into an anti-Jewish frenzy within days of taking power. In these occupied countries, where young men felt inadequate under foreign rule, the Jews were an easy target. The Germans didn't even have to do their own dirty work – locals were happy enough to stage pogroms, rounding up Jews for humiliation and torture. In Lvov, for example, a brutal pogrom took four thousand Jewish lives in the first week of German occupation. Later in the war, in Vichy France, a special French police division, the Milice, was formed in this unoccupied, allegedly "free" zone, specifically to hunt for and arrest Jews.

In Belgium the Germans implemented their anti-Jewish laws more slowly, but by September 1942 they had begun rounding Jews up for deportation. While initially claiming to be transporting these people to work details, the brutality of the roundups, and the inclusion of the elderly and the infirm, children and babies, made the deportations' sinister conclusions fairly obvious to anyone with the courage to face the truth.

In fact, the Belgian Resistance movement had sent a young man, Victor Martin, to Germany, as a spy in February of 1943. He was traveling on an academic pretext, but his true mission was to find out the fate of the thousands of Jews being transported by cattle cars to the east. He returned with the news "people are being burned." This first-hand information about mass extermination in German death camps confirmed the fears that those who were deported would not be coming back. His sinister report contributed to many Jews' decision to hide their children in Belgium. Victor Martin was eventually captured by the Nazis, but managed to escape from two different concentration camps, and to lead a normal life after the war.

After as many Jews as possible had been captured through mandates for "labor duty," the Nazis began making impromptu searches in the streets of Brussels. They would cordon off a city block and demand to see everyone's identification papers. Anyone with suspicious identity, and all Jews, would be arrested and brought to the Gestapo headquarters on Rue Louise for interrogation, torture, and then deportation. When the street raids stopped netting sufficient numbers, the Nazis began raiding Jewish neighborhoods, arresting people in their homes.

These roundups were terrifying. Gestapo stormtroopers, shouting and wielding guns, screeched into Jewish neighborhoods, pulling people from their homes, sometimes in their night clothes, throwing them into waiting trucks. Resisters were shot. Terrified Jews sometimes managed to throw their children over their backyard fences in an attempt to save them, begging their gentile neighbors for help. Some people killed themselves to avoid being deported. The exact number of suicides will never be known.

If the German soldiers did not find everyone on their list during the initial raid, they would usually return to the house later for a second sweep – so Jews who had successfully hidden or evaded the roundup and perhaps crept back indoors later were still at tremendous risk. Neighbors or friends who helped a Jew, if caught, would be either shot or sent along with the Jews for deportation.

The Nazis patrolled the Jewish neighborhoods and made random searches looking for escapees. The amount of energy put into this heinous effort is staggering. Finding and exterminating Jews was a very top priority in every country the Nazis occupied, from France to the Russian border, and from Scandinavia down to Greece, encompassing thousands of square miles of Europe. Hitler was determined to wipe the Jewish nation from the face of the earth.

The trucks carrying Jews, and other "unsavory" people arrested by the Gestapo, took the prisoners first to an internment camp. The Germans had built a "transit camp," a way station, for Belgian deportees in the city of Mechelen (Malines in French), located midway between Antwerp and Brussels, the two cities home to most of the Belgian Jews. From Malines, trains full of prisoners, called transports, each carrying a thousand people, left regularly for the killing camps, most to Auschwitz. A total of twenty-eight such trains, each carrying a thousand people, departed Malines with their human cargo between the summers of 1942 and 1944.

The Nazi commander of the camp at Malines until March 1943 was S.S. Major Phillip Schmitt. Schmitt was given this command by his Gestapo superiors as a reward for his outstanding work as commander of Fort Breendonk, a camp notorious for its poor conditions and brutality. Schmitt ran the Dossin Barracks, which housed the detainees at Malines, with particular harshness, making use of Jewish prisoners and of his vicious German shepherd to help. Prisoners were intimidated, beaten, and harassed mercilessly under Schmitt's tenure. After arrival at the camp they were "processed," stripped of their belongings, and forced to endure endless roll calls which entailed standing at attention in the courtyard regardless of the weather. Children were not exempt from these demands.

Prisoners were kept in overcrowded and terribly unsanitary conditions with scant food until the thousand-person quota was met. Then all thousand people – mostly Jews, some gypsies (Roma) – were loaded onto the waiting train, in cattle cars, and transported to Auschwitz. Almost none of the people deported from Malines survived. Most were immediately gassed upon arrival at Auschwitz. Some were kept alive for a while and used as slave labor. Most of them died too.

Hitler viewed Jews as a nation, not as a religious group. In his twisted philosophy, the religion someone practiced was irrelevant. Jews could not switch teams by converting. He came up with strict, if arbitrary, criteria about the percentage of "Jewish blood" that defined a person as Jewish. It was not only Orthodox Jews who were targeted. Secular Jews were too, as were people who considered themselves non-Jews, but perhaps had a grandparent who was originally Jewish. Non-Jews married to Jews were treated as Jewish if they remained with their spouses and children.

MELLY

A DESPERATE DECISION

It's hard to talk about what happened next. The summer of 1942, when Bobby was two years old, brought our ability to live like even half-normal people to an end. We Jews were being hunted by the Gestapo, rounded up on the streets, in our homes, roused from our beds, thrown onto trucks and sent away. We watched, aghast, as neighbors were brutally arrested. People we knew disappeared. We understood that being deported by the Nazis meant death. Every day could be our last.

One day this realization hit extremely close to home. Nathan, Inge, and Mama were living nearby, as I said. A few streets from them lived Mama's brother, Uncle Herman, with his wife Sally and their little boy Joachim. They had also left Chemnitz before the borders closed, and had relocated to Belgium. Mama and Herman were very close, and she was happy to have her brother so nearby. Her sister Sarah was in Brussels by now too. Some of Mama's other siblings had managed to get out of Germany before the war, but these were the only two in Belgium.

Uncle Herman was brilliant – a scientist and a businessman. He had developed some kind of special glue for fixing inner tubes. He had a little workshop in the basement of his apartment, where he worked to repair tires. By now most Jewish businesses had closed, so it was encouraging that Uncle Herman still had his shop. He was busy, and he needed extra help to run the place. Sometimes Mama and Nathan helped out with the business.

One day when Nathan and Mama were working in the basement atelier, there was a sudden loud pounding at the door. My brother went up and answered the door. The Gestapo. Where is Herman Fischer? they demanded. Nathan, not knowing what to say, pointed upstairs. The Gestapo pounded up to the apartment above. They did not ask Nathan for identification. My brother realized they were in terrible danger. He ran back down to the basement, grabbed Mama, and rushed her out the back door. Luckily his bicycle was right outside. Frantically instructing Mama to get on the handlebars of his bike, he took off as fast as he could, Mama perched perilously on the handlebars. There was a very steep hill right outside the building. Nathan had never been able to ride all the way up this hill without getting off his bicycle. But that day, adrenaline pumping and giving him superhuman strength, he made it to the top, even with carrying Mama on his bike as well. He pedaled them to safety. They got away from there before the Gestapo thought to ask them who they were.

But my Uncle Herman and his family were not so lucky. They never had a chance. The Gestapo barged into their home, ordered them all onto the waiting trucks, even their little boy Joachim, and drove off with them. They were transported to the camp at Malines and from there "east" into oblivion. We never saw any of them again. Mama was beside herself.

We realized we could be picked up any day; our chances for survival were dwindling. We had to think about saving Bobby. We had to hide him. I thought I had seen some dark times, but this –

planning to give up my child – this was a horror beyond my reckoning.

Down the street my mother also was in crisis. Inge and Nathan could no longer go to school. Inge was sixteen by now, she had a lot of friends, and one of them, a Christian girl, helped her get a job in a factory called Lustra. The factory made fur vests, and Inge would earn some much-needed money. It was good for Inge to have a job, and to have some kind of structure in her life. But Mama wanted to find a way to hide Nathan. Nathan was her pride and joy, her baby.

We all knew about the Resistance. There were people, Jews and non-Jews, who were clandestinely fighting the Germans. We heard that there were ways to get help, ways to hide Jewish children.

Can you comprehend the desperation we were in? Here was our choice: keep our child at home and know that, if we were captured by the Gestapo, as was likely, he would be killed along with us. Maybe we would have to endure seeing him killed before our eyes. Maybe they would torture him and make us watch. Or, we could give him up to strangers, knowing nothing about who would care for him, but hopefully saving his life. If we chose the latter option, it was likely he would grow up without parents, because it didn't look likely we would make it. The best possible scenario, the one we prayed for, was that the war would end, we would survive, and be reunited with our boy.

What made this decision even more heartbreaking was Bobby's young age. He was too little to understand what we were going to do, or why. There was no way to prepare him for what was coming.

With my brother Nathan, of course, it was easier. At fourteen, he was capable of taking care of himself, of understanding what was going on. He could communicate, he could make decisions. He didn't even seem like a child, although technically he was one. We knew Nathan could take care of himself.

But Bobby. Bobby was two. Thinking about giving him up made my entire body shake. I couldn't sleep, couldn't eat. Desperately I vowed that I would survive. I would not allow my child to grow up an orphan. So maybe Bobby saved my life. Because I was so low, so consumed by blackness, that I would likely have given up if I hadn't had my child to live for.

I can't talk about sending Bobby away. Forgive me. All I know is a young blonde woman came to the door. I didn't know her name. It was too dangerous. She spoke kindly to my child. We told him it was alright to go for a walk with this kind lady, and that everything would be fine. We kissed him and held him and tried not to show him our anguish.

And then Bobby was gone. I thought I would die. I didn't know a person could cry that much. At night I would wake up because Genek, the toughest man I have ever known, was sobbing beside me.

ANDREE GEULEN AND THE
RESISTANCE
SEPTEMBER 1942

The young Belgian Resistance fighter, working for the Jewish Defense Committee (the Comité de Défense des Juifs, or CDJ), went by the code name "Claude Fournier." Her charge that cool September day in 1942 was to pick up Alfred Bottner, aged two and a half, and convey him into hiding. She checked her notes. The child's nickname was Bobby. That would do as his code name. Best not to confuse the toddler more than necessary. She dreaded it when the children were this young. It was impossible for them to understand what was going on. She prepared herself for her errand.

Andree Geulen, a pretty Belgian girl born and raised in Brussels, was nineteen years old when the Nazis invaded Belgium in 1940. Although this invasion was hateful and disruptive, Andree was young and preoccupied with the details of her evolving life. And as a gentile, despite the Nazi occupation, she was able to complete her studies. She graduated in 1942 with a teaching degree in elementary-school education.

Very soon after beginning her first teaching job, to her horror, a few of her little students appeared in school with yellow stars saying

"Juif" sewn to their clothes. Until this point she had given little thought to the Jews' plight. Raised in a liberal family, she had never thought much about religion and was fairly oblivious to the growing marginalization of this population. She was vaguely aware of the Nazi anti-Jewish propaganda and laws, but it wasn't until this moment that she realized that innocent people, even little children, were being singled out for humiliating discrimination.

Appalled at this treatment of her young students, Andree decided to do something. Rather than allow some of the children to stand out with their badges of shame, she instructed all the kids in her class to wear aprons over their clothes. The children complied, and these aprons masked the yellow stars sewn onto some of the children's shirts. In her class there would be no talisman to mark the Jewish children as different from any of the other students.

Although the wearing of the compulsory stars was bad, worse was soon to come: soon Jewish children stopped attending school altogether. Perplexed and concerned, Andree, unlike some of her colleagues, started asking questions, even going to her students' homes to investigate. To her horror she learned that the children had literally disappeared, arrested by the Nazis together with their families and deported to concentration camps. The savagery of this Nazi outrage against fellow Belgian citizens made a huge impression on the young teacher.

When the Nazis first started rounding up Jews in Belgium in 1940 and 1941 they targeted only foreign-born Jews. The idea was to reassure the local populace that they were only clearing out "foreigners." Of course, this was a calculated ruse; by 1942 they were rounding up and deporting even Belgian Jewish families. Andree was appalled.

As the horrific roundups of Jews escalated in the summer of 1942, Andree met members of the secret Resistance movement. Wanting to do something to help save the children, she decided to join the underground effort despite the risks to her personal safety. And the risks were great. The Nazi regime demanded absolute obedience. Anyone arrested for potential sabotage against the Nazis could expect brutal and sadistic retribution. Yet many intrepid souls risked their lives to do whatever they could to undermine the hated regime.

One of her recruiters was a woman named Ida Sterno. Sterno was part of the CDJ, a small group within the Belgian Resistance devoted to helping Jews. Sterno realized that, with her affinity for kids and her blonde hair and blue eyes, Andree would be a perfect "escort," a courier to accompany children to safe houses. She was given the code name, "Claude Fournier," by which all her contacts in the CDJ, as well as the parents of hidden children, would know her.

Her job was to transport children from their families' homes to their hiding places. This was a dangerous job, and an emotionally wrenching one. Andree was given an address and some brief instructions. She arrived at a home and had to take a child, or two, often very young, away from their parents. Always she arrived to a scene of tearful separation. The little children would cling to their mothers. The older ones would often be the ones comforting their parents.

The pathos of these scenes can only be imagined: terrified parents sending their little ones into hiding alone, knowing they might never see them again. Yet parents were desperate to try to save their children if they could. Knowing the Gestapo could arrive any day to round them up, and that even babies would be taken, mothers and fathers hoped that by hiding their children they would save their lives. "Claude" never told the distraught parents where she was taking their children. She simply appeared at their door, and left again as quickly as possible, holding the child by the hand and walking briskly to the streetcar. She could not bring suitcases with her, as that would arouse immediate suspicion. So she sometimes made an earlier trip to pick up luggage, stowed it at the train station, and later returned to pick up the child. The parents had no idea who would take care of their child, or how they would manage, but anything was preferable to seeing them sent to a concentration camp.

A few times Andree arrived at a Jewish home while a roundup was in progress. Stunned neighbors watched in horror. Nobody could intervene. If a roundup was happening when she arrived she had to think fast, inventing excuses. More than once she had been questioned by Nazi soldiers, who demanded to know what she was doing in a Jewish neighborhood. So far she had gotten away with breezy responses and flirty looks. After all, she was an "Aryan" and allowed to move around the city freely. Sometimes she had to duck into a cafe in order to avoid confrontation with the German troops. If she had a child with her she pretended to be its mother or aunt.

At these times she experienced real fear. If the Nazis realized she was escorting Jewish children, not only would the little ones be seized and killed, but she would be captured and, as a member of the Resistance, brutally interrogated. But Andree was good at maintaining her cool.

Once they were away from the children's homes, Andree immediately started coaching them about their new identities, making them memorize their new names, emphasizing how dangerous it would be to slip up.

Once, while on a train, she had a six-year-old Jewish girl with her. She had coached this child: Your name is now Simone. You are not Sarah anymore, you're Simone. As it happened, another woman traveling on this train was taken with the cute little girl, and tried to engage her in conversation, asking the child her name.

The little girl turned to Andree. Do I tell her my real name or my new one? she asked.

Luckily this encounter did not result in disaster, but it shows how vulnerable the escorts were while transporting little children.

To distract the children, Andree sang them songs, gave them sweets, and made up stories and games to play during the journey. She would later describe how quickly she formed attachments to these little children, and they to her. It was doubly painful that she had to first wrench them from their families, and then quickly separate from them again when she dropped them off at their convent, home, or school.

Decades later, Andree would muse that it was her youth and the fact that she was not yet a mother herself that enabled her to carry out her job. Despite feeling deeply for the families giving up their children, it was not yet having experienced first-hand the strength of maternal love that allowed her to carry on with the work. Had she children of her own, she thought later, she would have broken down in the face of so much heartbreak.

This time, as always, Andree took a few minutes to make notes. The children, once separated from their families, had to remain in secret locations. As few people as possible were to know the child's true identity, or the parents' names. Yet if the war ended and the parents survived, there had to be some way for them to be reunited with their hidden child.

So, using a bookkeeping system she and some of the other escorts had devised – despite the risks – Andree kept a series of notebooks, each with limited information, hoping that it was sufficiently disguised should the books ever end up in the wrong hands. Andree managed to keep records that would ensure parents who survived would be able to find their children after the war. The books were kept in a safe house whose address Andree herself did not know.

This child, Alfred Bottner, would be given the code number 1068. The address of his family was in Rue des Ménapiens. The child would be hidden at a convent in Charleroi. Each of these demographic clues was kept in a separate notebook so that the information would be very difficult to put together. In one notebook Andree noted "Alfred Bottner – Child 1068," in another notebook, "Child 1068 – Rue des Ménapiens" in another notebook "Child 1068 – code name Bobby," in yet another "Bobby – Convent in Charleroi," and so on.

Once she had prepared herself, "Claude Fournier" took the streetcar to the address of the family. When she arrived she quickly introduced herself to the young couple and the little boy. She was relieved to see that Child 1068 was blond with blue eyes. That would certainly make him less suspicious-looking should prying eyes be on the lookout for Jewish children. As always, the child was apprehensive, and the parents distraught. While she felt very deeply for the parents, she knew that prolonging the goodbye scene would make everything worse. Briskly she told the boy that they would be taking a little ride on the streetcar. But the child did not seem to understand her.

She looked at the father. Does he speak French? The father shook his head. No, just Yiddish and German, he said. Andree bit her lip. If the child started speaking in Yiddish on the streetcar or on the train to Charleroi she could be in big trouble. Don't worry, the father told her. He knows not to talk. The mother looked stricken, tears running down her face.

The man bent down and whispered something in Yiddish to the boy. The child nodded and repeated the phrase.

Carrying only a small bag, "Claude" quickly left the apartment with the little boy clutching her hand, and made her way to the streetcar. True to his word, the child was silent during the ride. Smiling at him, she offered him a piece of chocolate. The boy's big blue eyes widened, and he accepted the candy and sat quietly beside her looking out the window. So far, this transport was going well.

Secrecy was necessary for everyone's safety. Andree and the other ten or eleven escorts, despite working together closely every day, never knew where their fellow escorts lived, and knew each other only by their Resistance code names. One escort, Paul Renarde, known in the movement as Solange, lived with her mother during the war. She never divulged her role as a child escort even to her own mother, claiming instead to be working for a legitimate Belgian social agency.

Where were these children hidden? Some went into private homes, joining families with other children, or were given to a young couple who wanted to adopt a baby; some were hidden in orphanages, and many were hidden in religious institutions.

Belgium is and was a Catholic country. In the middle of the twentieth century, monastic orders were still prevalent, and convents dotted the Belgian countryside. Their cloistered world made the convents perfect hiding places. Moreover, the German occupiers tended to leave these institutions in relative peace, ironically seeming to respect the Catholic convents as relatively sacred communities. Between two and a half and three thousand Jewish children were hidden in Belgium during the war. In addition, downed Allied pilots, Resistance workers, and other adults trying to evade the Nazis were hidden, off and on, within the convents.

Each convent housed a unique order – the Convent of Mercy, the Sisters of Saint Vincent de Paul, the Daughters of Mary, and others. These institutions were extremely hierarchical, each run by a Mother Superior. The nuns were used to obeying the Mother completely.

It was the Mothers Superior who made the decision about whether to shelter Jewish children when approached by desperate parents, by the resistance movements, or by the CDJ. It is not known what percentage chose to do so, but many did. Their motives seem to have been a combination of humanitarian ones (these children are in danger, they need protection) and a desire to "save" the souls of Jewish children through conversion to Catholicism. Once the Mother Superior had made the decision, the nuns unquestioningly did as they were told, incorporating the Jewish children into the structure of their particular order.

The Mothers Superior no doubt took their cues from the top. Cardinal Jozef-Ernest van Roey was the head of the Catholic Church in Belgium. Cardinal van Roey hated the Nazis, although his attitude toward sheltering Jews was less clear. He made some supportive statements criticizing the Nazis' racial laws, but as the war progressed he refrained from openly critical remarks. Still, it was important that the head of the Church was against the invaders and open to helping Jews. It is difficult to generalize about motivation, of course, and it is likely there were many complex reasons for agreeing to hide the children.

It seems that although the Nazis generally avoided confrontation with the Catholic Church, the nuns nonetheless perceived themselves to be at high risk of imprisonment, deportation, or death if discovered. And they were certainly aware that the children would be taken and deported if found out. The Germans did sometimes search the convents looking for Resistance fighters, or others on their wanted lists. So it was imperative that as few people as possible know about the hidden Jewish children. In the event of a search, a nun assigned to the task would have to whisk the Jewish children out of the building, hiding out in the woods or fields until the danger passed. This was especially important if the children looked Semitic. It was much easier and safer to incorporate fair-haired, blue-eyed children into the community. Dark-haired children with curls were in danger of standing out. There were instances of betrayal, when the children were denounced, but overall most of the hidden children (and occasional adults) managed to survive the war.

As soon as they were taken from their homes the Jewish children were given new identities and coached by their escorts to reveal only these new names, never their original ones, which were often traditional Jewish names. The nuns only knew the children by these new monikers. The children were forbidden to speak Yiddish or German, as those languages would mark them immediately as foreign and suspicious. As few nuns as possible were aware that some of their charges were Jewish. In fact, it was not unusual for even the children themselves to be unaware of other hidden children in their midst: the less said, the safer, was the philosophy. Bobby's beloved Uncle Nathan, for example, ironically was hidden in the very same convent at Banneux as Bobby would be later in the war. The toddler and the teenager were unaware of each other's proximity. It wasn't until after liberation that they discovered they had both been sheltered in the very same place at the same time.

Once sent into hiding, the children had to adjust to separation from their parents and families, adopt a new name, and deal with immense culture shock. Some, like Bobby, were plunged into a new language milieu. They went from living in families to residing in institutions, with the loss of privacy and comfort that accompanies that change. No longer did they have a bedroom, for example: they now slept in large dormitories. No longer did they eat meals around a small family table: they were now fed in an impersonal institutional style. Instead of being hugged, kissed, and adored by their mothers and fathers, they now had to take care of their own emotional needs. For the little ones especially, not old enough to comprehend the reason for this world-shattering change, the shock was extreme.

Added to the culture shock of being institutionalized was the deeply religious, extremely foreign world of the convent. Typically the nuns and their charges followed a strict monastic schedule. Waking early, after making their beds they then embarked on a long series of prayer services throughout the day. Almost universally, the Jewish children were forced to participate in Catholic prayers and to attend Mass. This was necessary to prevent the hidden children from standing out. It was also, at least in some instances, an attempt to convert them. Some hidden Jewish children were baptized, some confirmed – it is unclear whether by choice or against their will.

Children are great at adapting, however, and this new way of life eventually became the norm for them. At the end of the war, having adopted the Catholic traditions, the children were then again faced with the expectation to change overnight – this time to revert back into Jewish, even Orthodox, beings. Some of the hidden children had embraced the new religion and remained Catholic after the war, especially if they no longer had parents to return to. Others, like Bobby, hated the foreign religious ways, and shed them quickly and permanently as soon as they could.

The nuns had to find ways to house, feed, and care for an added influx of children, at a time when shortages were already the rule. Sometimes the Resistance sent monthly sums for the upkeep of the children. Sometimes families provided a stipend. This stipend would end, of course, if the parents were arrested and deported. Some of the convents had adjoining orchards or gardens and were able to supplement their food supplies from their own land. The CDJ was adept at forging ration cards, and these would accompany the newly minted identities of the children when they arrived in their hiding places, allowing the nuns to obtain basic rations for their charges.

To say the nuns worked hard would be an understatement. They had no domestic help. In addition to their daunting religious obligations, they were responsible for procuring food for the entire convent, cooking, cleaning, sewing, teaching, and caring for the children, as well as doing the farm work and taking care of the premises.

The survivors' recollections of the nuns are varied, which makes sense as these were individual people. Some recall warm relationships and fond experiences, others remember the nuns as cold, or even as harsh and cruel.

Bobby, Child 1068, was picked up by "Claude" in the dreadful late summer of 1942. Just as with the other children, she appeared at his parents' apartment and whisked him away from everyone and everything he knew. He was a little over two years old. He spoke no French. She spoke no Yiddish or German. But somehow she managed to bring the little child, now completely alone in the world, to his first hiding place, a convent in Charleroi.

MELLY
THE FAMILY DISPERSED

And so my family dispersed. Nathan too was sent into hiding. Everything was arranged by the Resistance; we were told very little. Later we found out that he was sent to a farm, up north, to live with a Christian family. The family needed an extra hand, and for a stipend they agreed to let Nathan live with them. I don't know if the farmers knew he was Jewish. Probably they suspected but didn't ask. At any rate, they weren't very nice to Nathan. They made him live in the barn. His job was to trap the moles that were feeding on the crops in the field. Nathan hated it there. Eventually he ran away.

Mama left Brussels too. She got a job as a housekeeper for a family she knew. The husband was Jewish – his name was Katz – but the wife was a shiksa. They offered to take Mama with them as a live-in domestic, and they left the city, moving to a village near the Dutch border. I rarely saw her. We didn't write; it was too dangerous. If letters were intercepted by the Nazis, or if collaborators got their hands on them, they could implicate not just our family but those who helped us too.

Collaborators were everywhere. You didn't know whom you could trust. It didn't matter how well you knew someone, or even if they were Jewish. People were so desperate to stay alive that they helped the Nazis by turning in friends and neighbors. So we lived in fear.

There was one infamous Jewish traitor, Jacques le Gros we called him, Fat Jacques. All the Jews in Brussels knew of and feared this man. His real name was Icek Glogowski. He was a Polish Jew like Genek. Before the war he had worked as a bouncer at a nightclub in Brussels. We all knew that his wife Eva and three young children had been arrested by the Gestapo in the raids in the summer of 1942. Eva, as well as nine-year-old Elka, seven-year-old Simon, and five-year-old Leon, were all sent "east" and killed at a concentration camp. Some said that Fat Jacques had actually denounced his own family, but I found that hard to imagine. What was true, though, was that this Jew switched his allegiance to the Nazis after his family was deported.

It's hard to believe that a Jew whose entire family had been killed by the Nazis would become a rabid informant, spending all his time hunting other Jews so they could suffer the same fate. Meshugene! This is how twisted our world became living under the Nazis. It wasn't bad enough that the Germans were hunting us; we had one of our own leading those mumzers straight to our hiding places. It was a hard and bitter life.

Fat Jacques roamed the streets of Brussels looking for people with Jewish facial features. He went to restaurants, cafes, stores, always on the hunt for Jews to denounce. He led the Gestapo to wherever Jews were in hiding, even assisted in their arrest, hitting Jews, pointing a gun, demanding jewelry and money. Of course the Gestapo paid him, and allowed him to live.

He was a stocky man in his forties. I guess hunting his own people let him eat his fill. He always wore a hat on his big head – a light one in the summer and a dark brown one in the winter. It was important to know what he looked like. I kept my eyes peeled for him every time I left the house. Sometimes he rode as a passenger in a Gestapo car, searching the faces of the pedestrians on the street, sitting alongside the dreaded Kurt Asche, the Gestapo officer in charge of the "Jewish problem" in Brussels.

Anyone Jacques suspected of being Jewish was arrested by the Gestapo and brought to their headquarters on Rue Louise for interrogation. Men were forced to drop their trousers. If they were circumcised they were brutally beaten by the Gestapo before being transported to the Dossin Barracks at Malines. Jacques le Gros was responsible for many Jews' deaths, that's for sure. I know for a fact that the CDJ tried to assassinate him on several occasions, but he managed to get away every time.

So I trusted no-one. I kept to myself mostly. I didn't chat with neighbors, I didn't make friends. I lived with Genek, and sometimes I saw my sister, but that was it.

Inge, as I said, was working at Lustra. This factory where she worked had been confiscated by the Nazis, of course, and the fur jackets assembled there went straight to the officers in the Wehrmacht, the German army. It shows you how bizarre our world had become. None of us thought twice about doing work to help the Germans. Nobody had any choice. Inge was happy to have a job.

She had been working at the fur factory for about a year when the Gestapo raided the place. This was in 1942, when roundups were escalating all over. Inge, seated by the window at her sewing machine, saw the Germans' trucks pull up in front of Lustra. Terrified, she ran into the bathroom. The Gestapo marched into the factory, demanding to see everyone's identification. They forced the Jewish girls to go outside, down to the waiting trucks. Inge heard the pandemonium from her hiding place in the bathroom, the yelling soldiers, the screaming girls, the gunshots, the crying.

Desperately she looked around the tiny bathroom. There was a small window above the toilet. Could she get it open? Would she be able to get through it? Where did it lead? Inge climbed up on the toilet and, trying not to make any noise, terrified that the Gestapo would hear her and run in to investigate, she pushed frantically at the window mechanism. She managed to open the window, and to hoist herself up. She shimmied through and saw that she could jump out onto the roof of the Lustra factory. She got onto the roof and ran, leaping from one roof to the next, all the way to the end of the block, and then down a fire escape. She kept running. Unbelievably, she managed to get away. All the other Jewish girls she worked with were captured that day by the Nazis.

Inge knew she was being hunted then. She was sure her name had also been on the Gestapo's list of Jews. She was afraid to go home, afraid that the Nazis would come to her flat and find her there. She was distraught by the raid at the factory, by her Jewish co-workers' terrible fate. But Inge was lucky; she had a very good friend. Friends were rare in those dark times, but Inge was always such a beautiful person that people adored her.

Anyway, this friend, Emma, who worked with Inge at Lustra, came to her rescue. I seem to recall that Emma's father owned the factory, but I'm not certain. At any rate, Emma had a small apartment in Avenue Chazal, and, after the raid, she let Inge stay there. Emma was not Jewish, and the risk she took by hiding Inge was enormous. But she did it. For most of the rest of the war Inge remained in hiding in Emma's apartment. Inge tried to pay Emma back by cooking and cleaning.

Usually this arrangement worked out fine. But sometimes there was a catch. You see Emma had a boyfriend, and when the boyfriend came to visit, Emma asked Inge to leave so they could have some privacy. Inge was in no position to argue, although she had nowhere safe to go, and felt completely exposed and vulnerable walking the city streets until she could return to the safety of Emma's apartment.

Sometimes when this happened Inge would come by to see me. For safety, we rarely got together, because we were conscious that we could be followed, and we didn't want to lead the Nazis to each other's apartments. But sometimes we did manage to see each other.

One day when Inge had to leave her hiding place she came over, and I noticed that she didn't look well. Her face was very flushed, and she was barely able to walk because she was so weak. When I put my hand on her cheek I realized she was burning up with fever. Inge, you're sick, what's wrong? I asked her. She said she had a sore throat and headache and felt very ill. I begged her to lie down, and she did for a little while, but then insisted on going back to her own apartment. Genek, usually impatient and angry when others were ill, was unusually solicitous of Inge, I noticed. Inge had that effect on people. He told her to stay with us for a while, but she refused. I don't know how she managed to walk back to Emma's, she really was in such bad shape.

A week or so later, worried, I decided to go visit my sister to see if she was recovered. She looked worse than before. She felt even more feverish, and she had a fine red rash all over her body. She said her throat felt a bit better, but that her joints really hurt. Also, she was having pains in her chest. I didn't know how to help her. There was no way she would go see a doctor: it was way too risky. She tried to reassure me but I realized she was very sick. I hoped Emma wouldn't kick her onto the streets in this condition.

When she eventually felt better, a few weeks later, Inge came back to see me. Her fever was gone, she said, although the chest pains were still coming and going. Emma had talked to her father about the symptoms, and they thought she might have rheumatic fever, Inge told me, which could damage the valves in her heart. We spoke about this for a little while – it sounded bad, and we weren't sure what it meant for her future – and then Inge stopped talking and looked at me carefully. Melly, she said, oh my God, Melly. Are you pregnant?

I was shocked. And then I realized that maybe Inge was right. I had been so despondent since Bobby was sent away that I hadn't noticed. I was barely able to function, so I hadn't paid attention to the signs: I was exhausted and nauseous all the time, and I hadn't been menstruating. I hadn't thought about it, really, assuming I was sick with grief. But yes, once again, I was in fact pregnant.

By the time I realized, it was too late to get an abortion. And anyway, the nice Jewish doctor who had done the procedures was gone, picked up and deported. I did find that out. Even if I had wanted to terminate, I didn't know where or how to do it anymore. So I had no choice. I continued on with the pregnancy.

I think I was in shock at this time. I could not process the loss of my little boy. Grief consumed me. I just couldn't believe that I had sent Bobby away for his own safekeeping and now was going to have another child. I vowed that this would be the last. The torment of imagining what Bobby was going through, wherever he was, was already as much as I could bear.

BOBBY
1942

The lady with the yellow hair was nice. She took him on the streetcar and gave him chocolate. That was fun. But she spoke funny, and he didn't understand what she was saying. Plus she clutched his hand too tight when they got off the streetcar. She walked fast too. He had to run to keep up with her. He wanted his mama.

But Mama said it was important to go with the lady with the yellow hair, so Bobby followed her onto the train. They sat by the window and the lady sang some pretty songs to him. He didn't understand what she was singing, but the music was nice. He saw a cow from the train window. He ate his chocolate. He sat quietly. Bobby nischt dreiden. He knew that was important. Don't talk, Bobby. He hoped he could go home soon.

After a while the train stopped and the lady took his hand and they got off the train. He didn't know this place. He felt a bit scared. But the lady smiled at him and held his hand and then they walked for a long time. At last they came to a big building and the lady knocked on the door. A really scary-looking person answered the door. At first he didn't know it was a lady, but then the scary person spoke and she had a lady voice. She had on a big black-and-white costume and you couldn't see her hair. She looked like a giant black-and-white bird. The lady with the yellow hair and the bird lady spoke to each other in that way he couldn't understand and they both kept looking at him. Bobby felt more scared. He really wanted to go home.

After a bit the lady with the yellow hair gave him a hug and then she left. Why was she leaving? He wanted her to stay with him. He wanted her to bring him back home. Now he was alone with the scary bird lady. She took his hand and they walked down some stairs. It was dark down here and Bobby started to cry. Shhhh! the bird lady said, putting her finger to her lips. Shhhhh! Bobby tried to cry more quietly. The bird lady spoke to him then, but he didn't know what she was saying. She looked kind of mad.

She brought him to another room where there were some other bird ladies. They all looked at him. They spoke to each other. Then Bobby noticed there was a row of beds in the room and there were children sleeping in the beds. It was very cold in this room downstairs and he needed to pee but he didn't know how to ask and he was even more scared. When would Mama and Papa come to get him?

Finally the bird lady brought him to an outhouse so he could pee. Then she brought him to a bed at the end of a row and she motioned that he should get in the bed. Bobby didn't want to. He didn't want to sleep here. He wanted to go home. But the lady looked mad so he climbed into the bed to wait for Mama and Papa. He was very hungry but the ladies didn't give him any food. The bed smelled kind of funny and the blanket was really scratchy but Bobby got in and waited.

The next thing he knew there were a bunch of faces staring at him and he didn't know them and he didn't know where he was and he wanted Mama. He looked around and saw he was in the bed in that dark room that the bird lady had brought him to. Did he sleep here? The faces surrounding him were young. They were children like him. Why were there so many children here? Where were their parents? Bobby curled up in his bed and tried to hide from the faces. The children just looked at him. Nobody spoke.

Then a bird lady came and she made Bobby get up and all the children walked to the outhouse and then to a big room with long tables and benches. The children sat down and he did too. They gave him a bowl and he saw that the other children were eating. He picked up his spoon and put it in the bowl of food. It looked maybe like porridge. Mama made him yummy porridge at home. But when he tasted it he didn't like this porridge. It was really bad. He put his spoon down. The bird lady came and knelt beside him and she tried to spoon-feed him the food but he turned his head and cried and wouldn't eat it. He was really, really scared now. He didn't understand where his parents were. They would never leave him in a place like this.

The children walked quietly back to the room with the beds. It was really cold and there was hardly any light and the children were very quiet. He got back into his bed and curled up in a ball. Sometimes he heard someone crying and then a bird lady would rush over and shush the crying child and then it would be quiet again. He tried to sleep but the bed smelt bad and he was itchy.

Bobby thought maybe he had been a bad boy and that's why Mama and Papa had let the lady with the yellow hair bring him here. He didn't remember what he had done. But he was sorry. He would tell Mama and Papa that he wouldn't be bad again. He really didn't like it here. He hoped they would come back to get him really soon. Or maybe Nathan would come get him. Nathan liked to go on streetcars. So maybe Nathan would get on the streetcar and come to get him and bring him home. Bobby waited.

Lots and lots of days went by. It was always cold and the food was always bad. They always had to be quiet. The only sound he heard was coughing. The children were always coughing. And crying too. The bird ladies got mad if the children coughed too loud or if they talked above a whisper. He could tell they were mad but he still didn't understand what they were saying. They never went outside, they never played, they never laughed. Mostly he stayed in his bed and slept. Soon he was coughing too.

He didn't like it here and he wanted to sleep until it was over. Bobby curled up in his bed and waited. He waited to go home.

BELGIUM AND HOLLAND
1943

It was a time of crisis. Nathan ran away from the farm where he had been placed for safekeeping and returned to Brussels. There he found that little Bobby was no longer at home; he too had been sent into hiding. And Melly, emotionally wrecked, was about to give birth again. Their mother Gertrude was in hiding with a family up north. Their father was still in the psychiatric hospital in Holland.

It turned out, although the family didn't know it at the time, that Leopold was in fact no longer at Apeldoornse Bos. In January 1943 the Gestapo invaded the Jewish psychiatric hospital and deported the entire thousand souls who lived and worked there. Even in a time of great horror the evacuation of this institution was marked by particular brutality. Many of the patients were quite compromised psychologically – developmentally disabled adults, neurologically impaired children, hallucinating people wearing straitjackets. Eye witnesses remember Nazis beating confused and frightened naked women with clubs. The Gestapo stormtroopers screamed at and violently pushed the bewildered patients onto the waiting trucks. The cold was fierce. Patients who fell to the ground were picked up and thrown like lumber on top of each other onto the trucks.

One eye witness, Dr. Jacob Presser, reported:

I saw them place a row of patients, many of them older women on mattresses at the bottom of one lorry, and then load another load of human bodies on top of them. So crammed were these lorries that the Germans had a hard job to put up the tailboards.

In the end, some patients had their fingers severed when the Nazis closed the truck doors on top of them.

The transport headed east.

Rudolf Vrba was a prisoner who later escaped from Birkenau. His job in the camp was the unloading of the new transport trains as they pulled in. He was at the camp when the transport from Apeldoornse Bos arrived. He gave an eye-witness report, recalling:

In some of the trucks nearly half the occupants were dead or dying, more than I have ever seen. Many obviously had been dead for several days, for the bodies were decomposing and the stench of disintegrating flesh gushed from the open doors.

This, however, was no novelty to me. What appalled me was the state of the living. Some were drooling, imbecile, live people with dead minds. Some were raving, tearing at their neighbours, even at their own flesh.

Some were naked, though the cold was petrifying; and above everything, above the moans of the dying or the despairing, the cries of pain, of fear, the sound of wild, frightening, lunatic laughter rose and fell.

The Gestapo asked the nurses at the hospital to accompany their patients as caretakers, and promised that if they volunteered to go they would be given the chance to return or to be reassigned to a new hospital. The nurses, almost all Jewish, readily came to their patients' aid, trying to comfort the frightened, alleviate pain, reassure. After the volunteer nurses were loaded onto the transport the Gestapo picked out most of the rest of the staff and made them get on the trucks too.

Rudolf Vrba recalls:

---

amidst all this bedlam, there was one spark of splendid, unselfish sanity ... nurses, young girls, their uniforms torn and grimy, but their faces calm and their hands never idle. Their medicine bags were still over their shoulders and they had to fight to keep their feet, but all the time they were working, soothing, bandaging, giving an injection here, an aspirin there.

Of course, the fifty nurses that accompanied their charges from Apeldoornse Bos did not return. They shared the fate of their patients.

The transport reached the Auschwitz-Birkenau camp on January 24, 1943, with 921 Jewish patients and medical staff, some of whom were children. Upon arrival, sixteen men and thirty-six women were selected to be admitted into the camp. The remaining 869 people were murdered in the gas chambers. Leopold Offner was one of those gassed upon arrival. He had been born in Auschwitz and he died in Auschwitz.

But the family in Brussels knew nothing about what had occurred at Apeldoornse Bos or of Leopold's fate until much, much later.

After spending about six months on the farm, Nathan fled and returned to Brussels in February of 1943. He had run away from the hiding place the Resistance had found for him. The farmers had treated him like a slave, forcing him to spend long back-breaking days in the fields searching for rodents and to spend his nights in the barn with the animals. They had not even allowed him to sleep inside the house as the cold of winter mounted. He had had enough. He made his way back to the city and found his sister Inge. Despite her own precarious situation she took him in.

Nathan was always close to Inge, and she doted on him. Melly was more aloof, more self-involved. Nathan did not feel as close to her. Nor did he feel much affinity for his brother-in-law Genek; the man was so much older than him, and they had very little in common. With his mother away, Nathan was happy enough to move in with Inge.

Inge was of course delighted to see him, but very worried about his return. She and Melly had promised their mother that they would keep Nathan safe. Nathan argued that he was as competent to take care of himself as his sisters were, more so probably, and he wanted to stay in Brussels. But so many people were disappearing by now that staying was out of the question. Inge contacted the Resistance about finding a new hiding place for Nathan.

Melly was preoccupied with her own problems. She was determined that this pregnancy would be her last. Despite the risk, she decided that she would have the baby in the hospital so she could make sure the doctors put an end to her fertility once and for all. On March 1, 1943, she went into labor. Genek could not accompany her to the hospital. He was so clearly a foreigner and a

Jew – it would be madness for him to come. Likely Melly told the hospital staff that her husband was off fighting, that was why she was alone. It was a plausible excuse; most men were off fighting at the front.

She used false papers to register at the hospital as a German woman, an Aryan. And although she screamed her head off during the delivery it was lucky that she swore in German. Nobody realized she was a Jew. Later that day Melly was delivered of a healthy baby girl. She begged her doctor to perform a hysterectomy. But maybe he did not feel comfortable doing so. She was only twenty-one years old. She pleaded with him to do something; she told him she couldn't feed another child, she needed contraception. The doctor may have eventually agreed to perform a tubal ligation, to tie her tubes, a relatively new procedure. Or perhaps he found another way to end Melly's fertility. Whatever the procedure, it seems that Melly did manage to convince the doctor to help her.

And so Melly went home from the hospital a few days later with her second child, Irene, in her arms, and with permanent birth control in place. It was March 1943, the darkest time in European history, when it seemed that hope was truly gone.

Melly and Genek immediately started making plans to hide this child too. They had to. Every day in Brussels could be their last. But this time they did not have two years in which to bond with their child, nor she with her parents. They would have only a few weeks, maybe a few months at most. Knowing that the baby would only be with them very briefly, Melly and Genek held their emotions in check. They loved her but they were preparing themselves for letting her go. Neither could survive a repeat of the grief they were enduring over sending Bobby away. They had to maintain some emotional distance. And so right from the onset there was distance between Irene and her parents.

And they were faced with an additional concern. If they gave Irene up, sent her into hiding, how would they recognize her when the war ended? Granted, it was a long shot that they would be reunited. But if they survived, how would they identify their tiny baby once she had become a little girl? She had no identifying marks on her. How would they know she was theirs?

Eventually they hit upon a plan. They would create a scar on her perfect little body. With a permanent mark on Irene, they would know that she was the right child if they came to find her years later.

Somehow they found a sympathetic doctor willing to help them. They brought the newborn to him and the doctor carefully made an incision on the baby's right thigh. It was about an inch long. He then sutured it back up, but not perfectly. He wanted a scar to remain. A week later he removed the stitches. Irene was left with a permanent mark on her thigh, one that could identify her to her parents in the future.

MELLY

A WARTIME BABY

One good thing happened in January 1943. I was maybe seven months pregnant with Irene and I was terribly depressed, so I remember this event because it really boosted my spirits. The most hated building in Brussels, the most terrifying place in this time of terror, was bombed! An Allied pilot flew a small plane over Brussels, and bombed the Gestapo headquarters on Rue Louise, shattering the windows, killing four Nazis and wounding many more. Then he let loose hundreds of Belgian flags that fluttered to the ground, a tremendous morale booster for his countrymen.

The hope this event brought us! We dared to believe that maybe the Nazis were not invincible, that the Allies could win this terrible war. I learned that the pilot was a Belgian named Jean de Selys Longchamps. He was flying for the English. Apparently he defied orders and flew his Hawker Typhoon airplane from England without permission, with the sole intention of bombing the S.S. headquarters in Brussels. We heard that the Gestapo had brutally tortured and killed his father, and he was determined to get revenge. So de Selys flew this plane over the city and discharged his entire load of bombs onto the detested building on Rue Louise.

English schoolchildren had colored Belgian flags, de Selys had stuffed them into a sack and brought it aboard his plane, and, after the bombing, he sent them flying down to the streets of Brussels as a sign of solidarity. The chutzpah! It was fantastic.

Of course the Nazis were enraged, and they sought retribution as was their way, rounding up innocent Belgians and executing them. But even so, this was a day to remember. We had almost forgotten that the Nazis were just people too, that they could be defied, killed. They were not invincible. I dared to hope that we would make it, that I would give birth to this baby, and then be reunited with my boy. Maybe we would survive this.

Later, when I lay in my hospital bed after giving birth, I heard more bombing. The Allies were getting closer. I heard anti-aircraft fire too, as the Germans retaliated against the Allied planes, trying to shoot them out of the sky. It was a fitting tribute to poor little Irene's birth in war-torn Brussels in March 1943. I gazed at this innocent child lying beside me and wondered if she would survive to adulthood, if I would be there if she did. And what of her brother?

When Irene was a couple of months old, before we sent her away, we got a message from the CDJ. It was the spring of 1943. Bobby was very sick. We found out that over the winter he had been hidden in a convent (much later we found out it was in Charleroi; at the time we weren't told anything). Now the nuns thought he was too sick to stay in hiding, they thought he was dying. They were sending him home.

My child was dying! My child was coming home! My emotions were all over the place. I was terrified and ecstatic, worried sick and breathless with anticipation.

Soon the same courier who had picked Bobby up six months earlier returned, holding our little son in her arms. He was pale as paper, thin as a reed, weak as a feather. But he was home. The escort spoke to Genek for a few minutes but I heard nothing, all my focus was on my little son. What was wrong with Bobby? What kind of illness did my child have? I held his emaciated little body in my arms, rocked him and wept.

Genek and I placed Bobby between us in our bed and prayed that he would recover. He stared at us with his giant blue eyes in his gaunt little face. I thought my heart would break. My poor baby.

But thank God Bobby got better. Within a couple of days he was eating, talking, even running around the apartment. Yes, he was undernourished, yes, he had an awful cough. But I think my child had been dying of a broken heart. He was too young to comprehend what was happening, too young to be separated from his parents and everything familiar. It almost killed him. And once he was back with his family he got well. I understood. My heart was breaking too.

I begged and made deals and scraped together every scrap of butter and sugar and flour that I could get my hands on. And it was tough to do, believe me. I took great risks. Crazy risks. But I needed to feed my son. Every day that I had enough ingredients, I browned butter, added sugar, then flour, then milk to make the sweet treat, papy farine, that Bobby loved. I wanted to feed him meat, eggs, something more substantial, but those items were no longer available. With joy I watched the color come back to his wan cheeks, and then some flesh return to his skinny limbs.

These were the few brief weeks when I had both my babies with me. I didn't want to sleep because I didn't want to miss a moment of this precious time. I wanted to cherish every second of having both my children home. Especially Bobby. I had missed that little boy more than words can express. I stared at him as he slept, memorizing his beautiful face. I even hired a photographer to take a family picture so I would have that as a memento. I tried to live in the moment, to ignore the warning bells going off in my head about how dangerous it was to keep these babies with me and Genek.

There wasn't enough money to feed us all. Even Irene was hungry; my milk supply was running out again. Genek's furs weren't selling. It was spring; nobody wanted fur coats. And anyway, people didn't have the money to buy even necessities anymore, never mind luxury items like fur coats. The Jews had disappeared, and the goyim were broke. Even the Germans were finally struggling; the war was dragging on, and the Germans were feeling the pinch too. Even Nazi officers were no longer buying fur coats.

The only way I was able to make ends meet was through illegal activity. I told you I took great risks. The black market was flourishing. People were desperate for food, and there were opportunities for those who were willing to risk their lives by smuggling contraband into Brussels. Remember, I was passing as a German Aryan. The Resistance had supplied me with forged documents. It was still insane to risk carrying illegal food supplies. Anyone who was caught by the Nazis could expect to be shot. We heard plenty of stories. But I didn't know what else to do. Genek couldn't do it, he couldn't pass as a goy. It was up to me.

So I started smuggling sugar. Every week I boarded the train out of the city and went to a rendezvous with a black market purveyor. No names. My job was to carry a few pounds of sugar in my bag and to deliver it to an address in Brussels. Every time I went I was given a new address: I never dropped the sugar off at the same place twice. I made sure to walk back to the apartment via a different route each time as well. I took the train back to the city. I went to the address and delivered the smuggled sugar, liquid gold in those days of rationing and hunger. I got paid when I made the delivery. I went home. I had money to buy my family food, also on the black market.

One day the worst happened. When I stepped off the train in Brussels a German officer approached me. My knees went weak. But I flashed him what I hoped was a friendly smile and said, Schönen Tag! He took my elbow and walked a few paces with me, chatting in high-class German. Then he asked me for my papers. I showed him the forged documents, my heart pounding. What if he realized I was a Jew!

I looked at his uniform. Wehrmacht. At least he wasn't the dreaded Gestapo. But still. I was carrying illegal sugar, and the punishment for this offense was death. And if he suspected I was Jewish I would be in the camp at Malines before the day was through. The officer handed me back my papers after a moment. He sighed. Miss, I need to see what's in your bag.

I stared at him. What to do? What to do?

Maybe it was that sigh before he asked to see what I was carrying, maybe it was some sixth sense, I don't know. But I had the feeling that this German might have a shred of humanity in him.

I was very young, only twenty-one, and he couldn't have been much older than me. I smiled, tossed my hair, batted my eyes. You know, sir, what young women carry in their bags, I said, feminine items. It would be very embarrassing for me to show them to you.

The officer stared at me. Well, miss, if it's too embarrassing to open your bag here on the street, perhaps you will feel more comfortable inside headquarters. He took my elbow again and started walking. He brought me to the German headquarters in Rue de la Loi. I was terrified. If only I could get rid of the bag I held, the incriminating bag full of sugar. I comforted myself by thinking that at least I wasn't being taken to Gestapo headquarters in Rue Louise. That was the most sinister address in Brussels. Nobody returned from that chamber of horrors.

Once inside the building the officer escorted me into his office. He asked me to take a seat. He looked at me quietly for a moment. Well, miss, let's take a look in your bag.

I was desperate. Whatever happened next, I had to make sure it only happened to me. I had to concentrate on not divulging that I had children, or where they were right at this very minute. Why did this have to happen when the children were not in hiding? Why, oh why, had I taken this risk? I took a deep breath.

Sir, I said, I'm going to tell you the truth. I am carrying sugar. I know it's illegal. I'm very sorry. I have never done anything like this before. But I was very hungry and ... well, I was just very hungry.

I expected, I don't know, a blow, a kick, maybe to be thrown to the ground. But the German just looked at me silently. I saw his eyes roam up and down my body. I had given birth just a couple of months earlier. My stomach was still swollen, my breasts full.

You're a German woman, yes? He said.

Yes. I was born in Chemnitz. I lived there until I was eleven, then my family moved here.

Ah, yes. I thought you were from Saxony. I am from Dresden.

We made small talk for a few minutes.

You're very beautiful, he said. I have not seen a beautiful German woman in quite some time. It is lovely to look at you. A pleasure to speak to you. Your accent reminds me of home.

I nodded.

You're with child?

I gulped. What was the right answer? Yes, I finally said.

So you are doing your duty, bringing a child into the world to serve the Reich.

Yes.

And you are hungry because you are pregnant, is that right?

Yes.

And because you are pregnant and hungry you smuggled sugar.

Yes.

Well. I think that the Reich would be best served by you carrying that child to term, do you not?

Yes. Yes, I do.

Then here is what we are going to do. You are going to leave that package on my desk. And then you are going to walk out of this office and down the hall and back out of that door we came in. Do you think you can do that?

Yes. Yes, of course. Yes. Thank you.

And you are obviously never going to do this kind of illegal activity again, am I right? Because if you do it again, my dear, you will get no mercy. Am I clear?

Yes, sir, you are. Absolutely.

Was this Nazi really letting me go? Or was it some kind of sick sadistic prank? I had heard stories like this. But I sprang up, removed the bag of sugar from my purse, dropped it on his desk, and practically ran out of that office, down the hall and out the door, onto the Rue de la Loi.

Once on the street my whole body started shaking. I had to duck into a cafe and lock myself in the bathroom until my trembling came under control. Had I really been picked up by a Nazi officer and then allowed to walk away? The closeness of this call was devastating. If I had been interrogated, tortured, what would I have said? How much would I have given away? Would I have divulged that I was Jewish, that my husband and children were right now in an apartment in Rue Rogier. That my sister and brother were in Rue Chazal? This was exactly why we weren't allowed to know where the little ones were hidden. It was too dangerous. And if that Nazi had known he'd let a Jew walk out of his door ... oh my God. I was afraid to leave the cafe, afraid of the street, afraid that I would be picked up again.

Eventually I made my way home to Genek and the children.

I told Genek the story. He was incredulous.

What? he kept saying. What? You were picked up and let go? How can this be? Neither of us had ever heard of such a thing. Melly, Melly, it's a miracle. A miracle.

And then we looked at each other and we both came to the same realization. The children were not safe with us. We would have to send Irene into hiding as planned. And Bobby had to go back too.

BOBBY
1943

He cried when he saw the lady with the yellow hair again. He ran to his room and tried to hide under his bed. But Papa dragged him out. Mama and Papa were both crying. They told him he had to go away again, but they promised it would not be the same place, this time it would be a nicer place, and it would only be for a little while, and they would visit soon. Please, Bobby, please, be a good boy. Go with this nice lady and don't make a fuss. Bobby could not stop crying.

The lady with the yellow hair picked him up and carried him outside. She gave him a piece of chocolate. Shhhh, she told him. He knew it was dangerous on the street. So he stopped making noise. On the outside. Bobby nischt dreiden. But inside he was still crying, screaming, Nooooo!

Once again there were streetcar rides and train rides, and once again she sang him songs and patted his head and smiled at him. But he knew she was bringing him somewhere bad and inside he kept crying.

The new place was just like the other one. There were children and they spoke funny and he didn't know what they were saying. There were bird ladies who watched the children but they weren't very nice. The food was bad and the blankets were scratchy and it was dark and cold and everybody cried and coughed.

Why, oh why, had they sent him here? Bobby curled up in a ball on his bed and waited for this to end, for his mama and papa to come bring him home. His world became very small, very dark, very quiet.

Days went by. Weeks went by. Months. Years.

IRENE

NAMUR, 1943

By now the attempt to save Jewish children was at its peak in Belgium, and despite the risks many outraged non-Jews joined with courageous Jewish men and women who were orchestrating this remarkable effort.

After Irene's birth the members of the CDJ and the Resistance responsible for placing Jewish children in hiding received notice that a newborn baby needed placement. This was a tricky situation – at only a few months of age she was too young to be placed in an orphanage or convent. This child would have to be taken in by a family. And that was tricky too. Because a family that suddenly acquired a new baby out of thin air could arouse suspicion, and would be at risk of denunciation. This placement would require some finessing.

The Resistance sent out feelers. A Catholic seminary student, Rene Bouchat, based in Namur, a city situated about forty miles southeast of Brussels, offered to help. Bouchat, a year prior to being ordained as a priest, was already active in the Belgian Resistance. As a Belgian he felt compelled to resist the invaders who were occupying his beloved country for the second time in his life. His home city of Namur had suffered terribly during World War One, and was suffering horribly again under the hated Germans. And as a man of the cloth he felt it was his duty to try to help the persecuted and beleaguered. So he aided the CDJ in finding hiding places for Jewish children whenever he could do so without arousing suspicion.

Rene Bouchat made inquiries about placing baby Irene. A few promising leads fell through. The CDJ was getting anxious. The child's mother had narrowly escaped being picked up. It was the summer of 1943. The only Jews still free were those in hiding. There was no time to lose.

Eventually, in desperation, Bouchat thought of his own parents. Would they be willing to take in a newborn? Mama and Papa were no longer young. They had raised him and his sister, and were now in their forties, happily leading a quiet life without the hubbub of young children. But Fernand and Marie-Antoinette Bouchat had been warm and wonderful parents, and they loved babies. Since he obviously would never be giving them grandchildren, maybe this child would fill a void?

Bouchat set out for his parents' house to talk to them. His only hesitation was about placing them in danger. He realized they would be safer if they didn't know the baby was Jewish. His parents were trusting souls. They had no practice in deception. He wanted them to be able to answer questions without hesitation. To have a candid story for their neighbors. He feared that if they knew the child was Jewish, and they were ever questioned by the Germans, they would not be able to hide the truth. And he would not be able live with himself if something happened to them. He hoped God would forgive this sin of deception.

As he walked he concocted a plausible story. He would tell his parents that she was a foundling, an infant abandoned on the steps of his church, presumably the illegitimate daughter of an unmarried girl who could not keep her. This had happened before. He would tell them that he had found the abandoned baby and was now searching for a good home for her. The more he thought about this plan the quicker his steps became. This was a good story. This could work.

Fernand and Marie-Antoinette were surprised at first. But as they considered the idea they warmed to it. Come to think of it, they would be happy to have a baby again. In this dreadful time of war and ugliness, it would be wonderful to have a child brighten up their lives. And they would feel good giving this poor abandoned little girl a good home. After all, the child was innocent of her parents' sins. Yes, they would take her, by all means. Bouchat urged them to think carefully about the responsibility of starting over with a newborn before they committed, but his parents had seized onto the idea and were not dissuaded.

And so in early June 1943 the intrepid Andree Geulen once again visited the Bottners' apartment and this time came away with a newborn girl named Irene. Melly and Genek (although Andree was not allowed to know their names any more than they could know hers) implored her to tell them where the child was going. But, following strict orders, Andree replied sadly that it was safer that they didn't know. Carrying the sleeping baby in her arms she hurried out of the building and walked toward the streetcar.

But she was not the only one engaging in a covert operation that day. As Andree walked to the streetcar, fifteen-year-old Nathan silently slipped out from a nearby building and, keeping a safe distance, trailed the young woman carrying his little niece. His sister Melly had begged him for his help. Please Nathan, please, follow Irene; you have to see where they take her. We have to know where our little daughter is going.

Nathan was a fair-haired blue-eyed German-speaking Jew, who might attract less scrutiny than some, but he was a Jewish boy nonetheless, and it was tremendously dangerous for him to be out in the street and traveling the streetcar. To avoid detection he traveled without the yellow star, but his papers were not in order. If he was stopped and questioned by the Germans he would be arrested. Jews were prohibited from riding the streetcar, but that was the least of his worries. If the Germans realized he was Jewish he would be sent to Malines and then deported, that was certain.

Nevertheless, Nathan followed Andree. He was sick to death of hiding. It felt good to finally be doing something useful for his family. He trailed the young woman and followed her onto the streetcar, keeping her in sight and then nonchalantly stepping off when she did. He followed her and the baby as they entered the Brussels train station. The young woman walked up to the teller. Nathan strolled by, positioning himself close enough to Andree to hear her ask for a ticket to Namur. Quickly he slipped into the neighboring ticket line and purchased his own ticket for the same train.

As the Namur-bound train pulled into the station Nathan followed Andree aboard. He sat at the opposite end of the compartment from her, pretending to study the scenery. He stole glances at the young woman, watching her coo into Irene's face, seeing her cuddle the infant when she fussed. The baby seemed content. Once, Andree gave him a hard glance, but he quickly buried his head in a newspaper and avoided eye contact for the remainder of the ride. The trip took about an hour. When they arrived in Namur he allowed Andree to exit first, and then he hopped off and continued trailing her. He was careful to keep in the shadows, far enough behind that she wouldn't notice his presence.

He trailed her through the streets of Namur. Andree approached a large church and went inside. As Nathan was about to enter after her he saw the young woman come back out of the church, this time without the baby. Was the child to be hidden in a church? Nathan was surprised. He had assumed a baby this young would be placed with a family. Before he had a chance to follow the infant, Nathan saw a priest hurrying down the steps. The priest was carrying little Irene in his arms. The priest headed down the street with the baby and after a few moments Nathan followed him.

The priest walked for a while, but finally turned into the gate of a small cottage and rang the bell. A middle-aged couple opened the door. They seemed excited to see him. The woman reached out for the infant and took her into her arms. The door closed behind them. After a while the priest came back out of the cottage without little Irene. He had left the baby with the couple. It looked like this was the hiding place.

Nathan made a mental note of the address and prepared to return to Brussels with the information that Irene was being hidden by a family in Namur. It would please his sister that these strangers were eager to receive the child. For better or worse, his sister Melly and brother-in-law Genek would now know the address of the family who had taken in their baby. God help them all.

Marie-Antoinette and Fernand were thrilled to be adopting a beautiful baby girl. She was sweet and mild-tempered, and as she got older she grew a mass of unruly light brown curls. With her hazel eyes and pudgy limbs she was the cutest child. They doted on her. Their daughter Rochelle, almost an adult, loved her too, and of course Rene came by to visit the child as often as he could get away from his duties. In 1944 Rene was ordained as a Catholic priest. Thereafter Rene, now Father Bouchat, led the Sunday Mass at church as his proud parents and sister and little Irene sat in the pews.

They all adored watching the child toddle around, prattling in her sweet voice as she learned how to speak childish French. Marie-

Antoinette dug out Rochelle's old doll carriage for the child, and little Irene happily pushed the toy around the yard as Marie-Antoinette tended her vegetable garden. The little one's favorite place was on Fernand's lap, pulling playfully at his mustache as he read her books and sang her songs. Just as they had hoped, having a child to raise brightened the bleakness of the war for the Bouchats. Irene completed their family.

Father Bouchat saw the bond forming between Irene and his parents. He was grateful that the child brought them so much joy, and relieved that she, in turn, was safe and loved. Sometimes he worried about what might happen in the future, but there were so many more pressing matters, so much work with the Church and with his clandestine Resistance activity, that he didn't have time to devote to what-ifs. Anyway, the chances of poor Irene's real parents surviving this terrible war were slim. Almost certainly the child would remain with the Bouchats forever. And that was good. No sense in worrying about things that were out of his control and unlikely to happen anyway.

Irene was loved and well cared-for by the only parents she knew as a baby and toddler. Her world, unlike that of her brother's, was a secure and happy place. Having been separated from Melly and Genek at only three months of age she had no memory of them, no knowledge of their existence. She was completely content growing up as the little Bouchat girl, the adored adopted baby of a loving Catholic family. These first two years of her life, ironically, would be the happiest of the next two decades.

PICTURES

Gertrude and her siblings; Uncle Herman is at the far left. Gertrude is standing on the right side of the picture

Last known photo of Beila and Yehudah Bottner,
1938

Genek's brothers - Joseph, Ephraim, and Moses
(Mundek), 1938

Leopold Offner

Gertrude Offner

Melly as a young child, Chemnitz

Inge, Nathan, and Melly; Chemnitz, Germany, c. 1930.

Inge and Nathan, c. 1939

Melly as a young adult

Melly and Genek on their wedding day, June 1939

Andree Geulen during the war

Page from Andree Geulen's books showing Irene
and Alfred Bottner at the top; Irene is two months
old, Alfred (Bobby) three years old

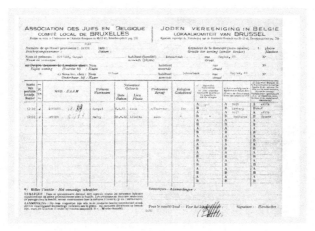

Registration form with the AJB for Genek and Melly

Melly and Bobby, 1943

Only known photo of Bobby in hiding in convent at Banneux;
3rd row from the bottom, 2nd child from the left

Irene, c. 1945

Genek, Melly, Irene, and Bobby, after the war, c.
1946

Irene and Bobby circa 1953, Montreal

Irene, 1962

Shoshana in the IDF

Nathan in the IDF

Genek in his fur store in Ottawa

Irene and Shoshana, 1965

Me and Inge, c. 1967

My mother with me and my great-grandmother
Gertrude holding my sister Sharon, c. 1967

Melly and Genek, 1984, 45th wedding anniversary

Me, my mom and dad, and my sister Sharon,
2013

Nathan and Soshana, 2016

Irene and Shlomo, 2016

My sister Sharon and her husband Rich, daughter
Alena, and son Jake

Me with my husband Danny, son Ari, and
daughter Sophia

Andree Geulen and Bobby, reunited after sixty
years

IN HIDING
BANNEUX, 1943

In January 1933, the very month that Hitler assumed power in nearby Germany, an eleven-year-old girl, Mariette Beco, living near the village of Sprimont in eastern Belgium, had a vision. Gazing out of her family's modest cottage window one winter evening she saw an ethereal lady bathed in a halo of light. The lady wore a white robe with a blue belt, her hands held to her breast encircling a golden heart. She beckoned to Mariette. The girl called to her mother to come outside to see, but her mother admonished the child for her overactive imagination, and locked the door.

The lady revealed herself again, however, in a total of seven visits in the ensuing weeks. No-one else was able to see the visions that Mariette described in vivid detail. The lady identified herself to the girl. I am the Virgin of the poor, she told her. Leading her to a nearby spring, she indicated to Mariette that a small chapel should be built there. She told the girl that the waters of the spring were holy, that these waters would cure the sick if the faithful believed and prayed very hard. Mariette was very clear about the message.

Mariette's family, though ostensibly Catholic, was not observant, and at first they scoffed at her visions. But the girl was adamant, and began attending church and discussing her visions with the local priest, Father Jamin. Her descriptions of the lady's appearance and the messages she received were quite convincing. Soon miracles began to occur in the village; the sick were indeed getting well. Mariette's family became devout believers. The villagers were amazed. Perhaps this young girl had really seen the Virgin Mary. Could their little village have had a holy visitation? A small chapel was soon erected by the community at the site.

As news of this holy visitation spread, the Catholic Church formed an investigative committee, sending its findings up the chain of command to the archbishop and eventually to the Vatican, and by 1937 a larger church was built near the Banneux Spring, as it was called, and pilgrims began visiting Our Lady of Banneux and praying for cures. In 1942 the Pope would authorize Our Lady of Banneux as a valid holy site.

The Holy Virgin's final appearance to Mariette Beco occurred in March of 1933, the very same month that the Offner family was fleeing from Fascist Germany. While Hitler was trumpeting the supremacy of the Aryan Nation, a little Belgian girl, Mariette Beco, was spreading the word of the Virgin Mary, saying that the Banneux Spring was "reserved for all nations, to bring comfort to the sick ... and alleviate suffering."

A decade later, during World War Two, more than one member of the Jewish family who had fled Germany would find refuge at Our Lady of Banneux, hiding out in the church in an attempt to survive the Gestapo's ruthless annihilation of the Jewish race.

By 1943, with the only Jews still living in Belgium in hiding, the Nazis were no longer able to fill their quotas for deportation. They issued a declaration urging all Jews in the country to return to their homes, to resume their normal lives, stating that the anti-Jewish actions were over. Of course, this was a ruse; any Jews foolish enough to believe the mandate were summarily picked up by the Gestapo and deported.

It was at this time that the Resistance, particularly the CDJ, escalated its attempt to hide as many remaining Jewish children as possible. The effort was aided by a number of brave and committed non-Jews who risked their lives to do what they knew was right.

One vital participant was Albert Van den Berg, a non-Jewish lawyer active in the Belgian Resistance. He was instrumental in helping to hide children in the Banneux area, where Bobby and Nathan were both eventually placed. Sadly Mr. Van den Berg was arrested by the Nazis in 1943 and sent to a series of prisons and concentration camps. Brave and uncowed to the very end, he is said to have declared as he was being led away by the Gestapo, "la vie est belle!" Tragically he died just before liberation in Neuengamme camp. Forty years after his death his efforts in saving 300 Jewish children were honored by the State of Israel: Albert Van den Berg was awarded the honor of Righteous Amongst the Nations. It is thanks in part to Mr. Van den Berg that the infrastructure and funds existed to hide the children in the area.

So, it was to the convent at Banneux that two-and-a-half-year-old Bobby was sent by the CDJ, where he was sequestered away for the second time, in the basement. He was one of scores of little boys living in that subterranean world of damp earth and loneliness, watched over by overworked Catholic nuns whose job was to keep the children alive, not to mother them. Bobby never found out how many of these children were hidden Jews and how many were Catholic orphans.

Nathan's stay in Brussels had been brief. He had managed to follow his niece Irene as she was sent away, but soon after that, in the summer of 1943, his family insisted that he go into hiding again too. By now Nathan spoke good French. This was important as he was able to blend in as a Belgian Christian much more easily once he spoke the language.

For a few months Nathan lived, along with a half-dozen other boys, in the home of a priest in Namur. This was a temporary hiding place. When it became too dangerous to stay there, Nathan was relocated by a Benedictine monk called Pere (Father) Bruno. Father Bruno, born Henri Reynders, was actively working with the CDJ and Albert Van den Berg to hide Jewish children from the Nazis. He ran a virtual underground railroad, finding hiding places, communicating with the Resistance, and frequently transporting the children into hiding himself. A tall thin prematurely bald man with a kindly smile, sporting round eyeglasses with dark frames, Father Bruno risked his own life throughout the war. Luckily he survived. He too received the honorific title Righteous Amongst the Nations from the Israeli government decades later for his heroic efforts in saving 400 Jewish children.

And so Father Bruno brought Nathan to a new hiding place, this one a monastery in Banneux. Nathan came to live in hiding at the Banneux Spring, the site where Mariette Beco had famously seen the Virgin Mary, and had directed that the place be "reserved for all nations ... to alleviate suffering." By this time he was fifteen years old.

So Bobby's beloved Uncle Nathan had come to live at the same institution as the lonely child. How different Bobby's experience might have been had he had Nathan to visit him and give him some much-needed affection. But the two were unaware of each other's proximity.

Nathan was assigned a new name. From now on he would be known as Nestor van Haverbeke. As was often the case, he was allowed to keep his first initial, but the rest of his name was changed to a typically Belgian one. Father Bruno made sure the boy had the necessary documents and forged ID cards before bringing him to his new hiding place.

Nathan joined a group of orphaned teenage boys living at the monastery. He did not know if any of the other boys were Jews in hiding like himself. He knew better than to ask. His job was to blend in and avoid calling attention to himself. His survival depended on it.

These older boys' lives were very different from those of the little ones like Bobby. These teenagers had a "legitimate" reason for being there: they were orphans, cared for by the Church. They were not confined to the basement. They spoke French and went to Mass. They lived openly as wards of the Church – attending classes, doing their chores, and eating their communal meals, allowed to walk the grounds, speak normally, and socialize with each other. In addition, they were old enough to understand why they were there; they knew that they were much better off in the safety of the convent than any of the alternatives. Many young men were off fighting in the war; these boys were not quite old enough to fight, but they were certainly old enough to realize that they were lucky to have a place to keep them safe. And they were old enough to get along without their families, able to deal with institutional life without it decimating their psyches.

And so Nathan immersed himself in the rhythms of monastic life. Certainly it was easier than the farm that had been his first hiding place. Nathan went along with the others as they genuflected and crossed themselves, and hoped none of the boys or priests would realize he was not as well versed as the rest in the rituals of the Mass.

One day the head priest tapped Nathan on the shoulder. Nestor, follow me, he said, let's take a walk, I want to talk to you.

Nathan hoped he wasn't in trouble.

They walked through the grounds of the convent for a while in silence.

Father, what do you wish to talk to me about? Nathan asked.

The priest kept walking. Finally he said, I have a question for you. Do you come from a religious family?

Nathan was taken aback. His lack of experience with the Catholic Mass must have shown.

The priest continued to walk. Nathan kept pace, wondering what to say.

Look, the priest said, turning to face Nathan, I know exactly who you are and I know why you are here.

And now, thought Nathan, this is the end. My time is up. If the priest knew he was Jewish, he would turn him in. Harboring Jews was a capital offense. Everyone knew this. This priest would denounce him. He would be arrested, sent to Malines, deported. He would never see his parents again.

So tell me son, I want to know, do you come from a religious family?

Nathan thought of his father, of the years spent studying Torah and Talmud at the kitchen table in the cottage in Holland. He thought about his father's desire for him to become a rabbi. Yes, he replied, I do.

Good, said the priest. And do you believe in God, Nestor? he continued.

Yes.

Good. That is what is important.

The priest was silent for a few moments. I have prayed on this, he said presently, and I do not think it matters if you worship God in

134

one way or another way, what matters is that you believe. That you believe in God. Yes?

Nathan nodded. I do, Father.

Good, continued the priest. God is merciful and He loves his children. You know this, you have been raised right. Your parents taught you. Your God is the same as our God, yes? And God brought you to us for a reason. We will shelter you here. We will not let harm come to you.

Nathan blinked. Yes, Father, thank you.

I believe God wants us to help you, Nestor, continued the priest. You are doing fine, son, he went on, I want you to keep doing what you have been doing. I want you to keep attending church, go to the Mass. It's fine that you don't take Communion, that is no matter. You are a good boy, you believe in God, and so we will take care of you. Don't be afraid.

They walked back toward the shrine. The priest patted Nathan on the shoulder. Go on back inside, son. Your secret is safe with me.

Nathan never knew how the priest found out he was Jewish. Maybe it was his looks, maybe his accent, maybe his lack of expertise with the Catholic prayers, maybe all of the above. But, true to his word, the priest made no further mention of Nathan's heritage. He did not denounce him to the authorities. He did not turn him in to the Germans.

Nathan continued to live quietly and safely in Banneux. Unlike Bobby he was not traumatized by this experience; he did not suffer sensory deprivation or crippling loneliness; he was not kept in virtual darkness; he was not forced to be silent. The food was adequate, if non-kosher. He did not like living like a Catholic, but compared to the alternative it wasn't so terrible. He went along with what the other boys were doing, and he too waited.

BACK IN LVOV
1939-1943

Genek stopped hearing from his family. His letters went unanswered. He knew nothing of what had happened to his parents, his brothers, cousins, aunts, uncles, his many friends, classmates and team-mates. Last time he had seen Lvov had been in 1936. His home city of three hundred thousand people had been one-third Jewish then. What had happened to these hundred thousand Jews? The Nazis had invaded Poland in 1939 and in fact, unbeknownst to Genek, there were probably double that number of Jews in Lvov after the invasion, as refugees from Germany and Poland fled into Ukraine.

Galicia, the part of Ukraine containing Lvov, was in constant flux – due to its location, the area was the fulcrum in a never-ending political tug-of-war. Russian, Polish, and Ukrainian nationals fought ceaselessly over the area. Starting in 1938, right before World War Two, the Russians were in charge. On September 1, 1939, the Germans invaded Poland, launching the war. Just twelve days later the German army reached Lvov and put the city under siege. By the end of the month, however, the Russians were back in control.

The Nazis and the Soviets came to an uneasy truce at this time, dividing the control of Poland and Ukraine between them. The Soviets controlled the Ukrainian part of the country, forming a state called the Ukrainian Soviet Socialist Republic. The Jewish community in Lvov was initially delighted to find itself on the Russian side of this divide. But this delight was short-lived. The Soviets began deporting Jews and Poles eastward as forced laborers almost immediately.

It is ironic that Stalin's government, virulently antisemitic, would inadvertently save over two hundred thousand Polish Jews' lives. Beginning in 1940, the Soviets deported over a million Poles, including Jews, into remote areas of the Soviet Union as slave laborers. Many of these men worked under grueling physical conditions in Siberia and Eurasia. However, some of these Jews survived the war; they were some of the only Polish Jews who did. The rest, over three million Polish Jews who were not deported by the Soviets, perished in the Holocaust.

On June 22, 1941, the Nazis re-entered Galicia and ousted the Soviets. Approximately ten thousand Jews managed to escape Lvov right before the Nazis took over, choosing to join the Red Army as the lesser of two evils. Genek's youngest brother, Mundek, was one of these Jews. The lad signed on as a soldier for the Russian army, realizing his chances were slim either way, but perhaps better as a Russian soldier than as a civilian under Nazi rule.

In June 1941 he boarded the train shipping the new recruits eastward toward Russia. Mundek's last memory of Lvov was of watching his father Yehudah, crying and waving, running after the train carrying him and the other soldiers out of the city. Mundek never saw his father, or any of his family other than Genek, again.

When the Germans took control of Lvov they renamed the city Lemberg. Despite its now-German name, however, the city continued to be a hotbed of opposition, and strife between ethnic groups. The streets erupted in violence between Ukrainians, Poles, Jews, and Germans. Even the brutal Nazis had a hard time retaining order. The Nazi regime decided to give the people a common enemy.

The Germans circulated a rumor that the Jews had executed Ukrainian political prisoners. This rumor sparked massive pogroms by Ukrainian nationals living in Lvov, as well as support for the killing of Jews by Einsatzgruppe C.

The Einsatzgruppen were mobile death squads composed of German Secret Police (S.S. or Gestapo). These battalion-sized squads travelled from city to city right behind the advancing German army. Their express directive was to kill all "undesirables" in the area the army had invaded. The squads were supported by vans carrying food and ammunition, just as any fighting force would be. They were very well organized. There were four main squads, A,B,C, and D, each assigned a specific area of Poland and Ukraine. As they reached a city, the S.S. rounded up the "undesirables" – mostly Jews, some Roma, some political prisoners – and marched them to predesignated killing sites in the nearby forests. The victims were forced to strip, hand over all their valuables, stand at the edge of a mass grave, and wait to be shot. Sometimes the victims were forced to dig their own graves prior to being murdered. At first the Einsatzgruppen targeted mostly Jewish men, but soon included women and children in this ghastly execution scheme. By 1943, the Einsatzgruppe squads would kill over a million people, mostly by shooting, and later in mobile gas vans.

Within two weeks of the Nazis' arrival in Lvov, four thousand Jews had been murdered in the streets in massive pogroms. Countless more were shot by the roving death squads. There is no record of exactly how many people were killed, or where, by Einsatzgruppe C, as the squad carried out its demonic deeds in the city.

The following month another pogrom called the Petilura Days resulted in another two thousand Jewish murders in Lvov in just two days. Women were raped, men were beaten, synagogues were burned, Jewish businesses were destroyed and looted in an orgy of violence.

By July 8, 1941, Jews still in Lvov were forced to wear the yellow star, and by the end of that month a Jewish committee, a Judenrat, was formed at the behest of the Nazis controlling the city. This committee was headed up by Dr. Josef Parnes. Dr. Parnes and the rest of the Judenrat were a guise under which the Nazis could control the Jewish population, just like the AJB was in Belgium.

In August 1941 the Nazis demanded that the Jewish population of Lvov pay a ransom of a staggering twenty-million rubles. The understanding was that paying this ransom would protect the Jewish community from harm. The Nazis took many Jews as hostages to ensure that this sum would be raised. Somehow the Jewish community was able to collect enough funds to pay this enormous fine, on time, but once the Nazis had received the ransom they killed the Jewish hostages anyway. In October 1941 Dr. Parnes was also killed because he was not cooperative enough with the "handing over" of Jews for deportation to the Janowska concentration camp. He was quickly replaced by another prominent Jew.

In November 1941 the Germans established a ghetto in Lvov, relocating tens of thousands of Jews into a small area surrounded by barbed-wire fences, where overcrowding, disease, and malnutrition were the rule. Some five thousand sick and elderly Jews were killed during this relocation, by Nazi soldiers and by Ukrainian hooligans who hated the Jews as much as the Nazis did. Many more Jews subsequently died in the ghetto due to the abysmal living conditions. The ghetto was periodically raided by the Nazis, who seized Jews for deportation, or killed them right there in the ghetto.

Following the raids, the Jews still living outside the ghetto were then forced to move in. There were periodic attempts by the Lvov Jews over the next years to resist and fight, but, with few exceptions, these efforts were quickly and ruthlessly quashed.

Next came the mass deportation of Jews to labor camps and to concentration camps. The Belzec camp received over fifty thousand Jews, and Janowska camp was a close second-place recipient.

The Lvov ghetto lasted about two years. In 1943 the Nazis "liquidated" it, sending any remaining survivors to Auschwitz or other killing camps, or marching them into the forest to be shot.

Of the original hundred thousand Jewish inhabitants, as well as an additional hundred thousand Jewish refugees who had moved to Lvov prior to the Nazi occupation, only a handful were still alive when the Lvov ghetto was destroyed in late 1943. Even fewer were alive when the Soviet Army liberated the city in 1944.

Among those who perished were Yehudah and Beila Bottner, and two of their four sons, Joseph and Ephraim, as well as grandparents, scores of aunts, uncles, and cousins, and hundreds of friends. Old people, young ones, children, babies, all were gone. Religious, secular, Hassidic, Zionist, agnostic, atheist – it made no difference. If they were Jewish they were doomed. There are no known records of precisely where and when the Bottner family died. Probably they were either killed in a pogrom, shot in the killing fields around Lvov by the Nazis, or deported to Belzec concentration camp and killed there.

Yehudah and his two sons did survive long enough to relocate to the Lvov ghetto. Work cards with their names on can be found in the archives in the Holocaust Museum. But Beila (Berta) disappeared – perhaps she died of natural causes, perhaps she was killed in a pogrom or in the relocation process. The very last communication from her was in April 1940 in a telegram. Genek had sent his parents notification of little Bobby's birth and Berta replied via telegram, sending congratulations. Genek's one solace was that his parents did know they had a grandson. They would never meet him, but Genek would later say that he hoped it had brought them a little joy.

The only survivors of the family from Lvov were those who had left: Gimpel (Genek), who had fled to Belgium years earlier, and Moshe (Mundek), who had joined the Red Army.

Mundek fought as a soldier for the Soviets for a couple of years until he was wounded by a gunshot to the arm. He received treatment in the Soviet city of Rostov, east of the Black Sea, some 850 miles from his hometown. The shot caused a serious wound, and he barely managed to avoid amputation.

Unable to rejoin the fighting after being wounded, Mundek was no longer useful to the Soviet army. He was told that as a Jew he had two choices: go to prison, or go to Siberia to work in the coal mines. Mundek chose "Siberia," a euphemism for the vast hinterland of the Soviet back of beyond, and was sent to work in Kazakhstan.

Although he was a virtual slave laborer, he did meet the woman he would marry, Yetta Herscovitz, a Romanian Jewish refugee who had also fled to Kazakhstan. They managed to get married and somehow survived the war. After liberation they would find their way back into Central Europe. Mundek wanted to return home to Galicia, but Yetta was afraid of returning to Lvov, having heard stories of the Ukrainians' brutality toward Jews. They would eventually make their way to a refugee camp in Tyrol where their only child, Golda Bottner, would be born in February 1947.

It was in the refugee camp that the two surviving brothers would eventually be reunited. After liberation, Genek would make frantic, endless inquiries about his missing family, coming up with nothing about his parents or other relatives. Two years of searching would yield nothing. The family was gone, and no-one knew how or where. Eventually he would find his brother Moshe's name on a Red Cross list. Genek would set out to find the only member of his family who had survived the Holocaust. He would convince Mundek to return with him to Belgium along with Yetta and Golda, and help him get apprenticed in his own field as a furrier.

GENEK'S LUCK RUNS OUT
BRUSSELS, 1943-1944

After the children were in hiding, Melly and Genek made a pact. If someone denounced them, their dwelling would be under surveillance; it would be unsafe to re-enter their apartment. If one of them were to disappear, how would they ever make contact again? There was no way to telephone each other, nowhere they could leave a message. They needed to have a place to reconnoiter if separated. They came up with a busy street corner in the center of Brussels, and a time of day, late afternoon. If one of them disappeared, the other would go to this street corner every day at four o'clock. They would try to reunite this way.

Considering the overwhelming chance that if one of them was picked up he/she would be promptly deported, this was a very optimistic plan. Those who disappeared in occupied Belgium did not return. But they made this pact, and vowed to keep it. They had two young children out there who needed them. They had to survive.

For now they avoided repeating patterns, tried not to have habits that would make them predictable. They took different routes every time they left the apartment. They went out at varying times of day. Eventually they rented another apartment so that they would have multiple addresses, multiple potential hiding places. They randomly chose where to sleep every night – some nights in Rue des Menapiens, some in Rue Rogier, some elsewhere. If anyone was watching them, following them, they wanted to be as unpredictable as possible.

Melly later found out that the couple who rented the apartment underneath theirs was terrified of them. Because they heard Melly speaking German, and noticed her erratic patterns, they assumed she was a German informer. They thought most likely she was Gestapo, sent to live among the Belgians to gather intelligence. Ironically this was a great help in keeping them safe. If the neighbors thought they were Gestapo, it was unlikely anyone would denounce them as Jews!

For a time they managed to get by, Melly doing most of the errands, Genek staying indoors, especially during daylight hours. Of course, there was a curfew, but if he had to go out he tried to go when the light was dim, and he wrapped a scarf around his lower face and pulled his fedora down as low as he could. He looked like a Jewish man, and he risked his life every time he left the apartment. Jacques le Gros and other informers were always on the lookout for someone to denounce; the Nazis were always on the prowl for someone to fill their quotas for deportation.

But one day Genek's luck ran out. He was stopped on the street by the Belgian police and asked for his documents. He was carrying a false ID, of course, stating that he was a Christian. But the police were suspicious of his looks and his accent; they suspected he was an illegal immigrant. They turned him over to the Wehrmacht. Somehow, miraculously, he was not sent to Malines for processing and deportation to Auschwitz. At this point in the war the Germans were desperate for laborers to keep their war machine going. Instead of being killed or deported, Genek was assigned to work as a forced laborer in a factory.

The Germans used forced labor (slave labor) in every country they occupied. Most of these laborers were transported from their own countries into Germany to work in factories, agriculture, or construction projects. Two hundred thousand people were conscripted from the tiny country of Belgium alone. From larger countries, many more people were seized and sent to work as slaves. Slave labor was a mainstay in the Nazi economy; millions of people were used as slaves by the Nazi regime during the war. Jews and other subhuman undesirables were worked literally to death, but other prisoners served as free labor as well.

The Nazis, as was their way, categorized their slaves by strict racial criteria. Jews and Roma were at the bottom of the ladder, subhuman, deserving of no mercy, as little food as possible, and to be worked until they were dead. They were treated worse than animals. Slavs (Poles and Russians) were one small rung up and were treated very slightly better; Czechs were a little higher still. The Dutch were considered to be of a higher class and their work conditions reflected that status. "Nordic" people like the Scandinavians were considered to be closer to Aryan, and were treated much more favorably.

At the beginning of Nazi occupation, Belgium had been ordered to select ten percent of its work force to aid the Nazi war machine. But as the war dragged on, the Germans conscripted as many able-bodied men and women as possible, usually transporting them back into Germany to serve. Sometimes, however, factories that were producing goods for the German army in occupied countries needed staffing too. And it was to such a factory within Belgium that Genek was sent in late 1943.

It is not known which factory he was sent to, or the exact date, but he would later tell Bobby of the three months he had spent working as a forced laborer for the Nazis. He was a skilled furrier; most likely the Germans took advantage of this skill and had him working in a garment factory, probably helping to sew uniforms for German soldiers. It is possible he worked at Hugo Boss, a clothing company that made Nazi war uniforms, that would later become a fashion giant. The only reason he was not killed or sent to Malines and then to Auschwitz was that somehow he avoided being recognized as a Jew. He probably passed as a Christian Pole.

And so Melly was left alone, children in hiding, husband gone. She had no idea what had happened to Genek, whether he was still alive, whether he had been deported, detained, or arrested. Fear and despair were her constant companions. But she stuck by the promise she and Genek had made. Every day at four o'clock she made her way to the street corner they had designated as a rendezvous site. Every time she went there she was terrified of being arrested. She walked up and down the street a couple of times, trying her best to avoid notice. She was convinced it was a fool's errand. But she did it nonetheless. Every day when Genek failed to appear she carefully chose a new path back to one of her lodgings, trying to look casual as she glanced behind her, hoping she was not being followed.

Genek, meanwhile, spent three months as a virtual slave. The workers were given little food and very little rest. Their hours were long, from before dawn until well after dark, seven days a week. They lived in abysmal conditions in cold, damp, rodent-infested cramped rooms. Their Nazi slave masters forced them to stand at attention for hours for roll-call, beat them with riding crops if they didn't move quickly enough when ordered to do something, and demanded unquestioning obedience. They were given work quotas and were threatened with beatings, or worse, if they didn't meet them.

Genek kept his mouth shut and his eyes open. He knew his worst-case scenario was attracting too much notice. If the Nazis realized he was Jewish they would surely kill him. He sat at his sewing machine and churned out the garments as he was told to do. He watched the guards. He noticed the way they carried themselves, the arrogant posture, the way they tucked their riding crops under their arms, goose-stepping in and out of the factory, shouting Heil Hitler! He made note of times when the guards stepped away to share a cigarette and to make disparaging remarks about the prisoners. He said very little. He didn't care about the conditions, the hunger, the cold. He studied the environment and bided his time, waiting for a chance to make a move.

One day the guard in charge put his crop down and headed off whistling toward the latrine. Genek knew this guard would usually stop and have a cigarette with his friend after he had used the toilet. He figured he had maybe a five-minute window. He wasted no time. In a flash he was up, grabbed the riding crop the guard had put down, tucked it into his armpit as the Germans did, threw back his shoulders, and goose-stepped toward the factory door. Nobody noticed him. The laborers kept their heads down. In their peripheral vision they would have seen the typical Nazi guard stance and posture, not a prisoner trying to escape. Genek kept going until he reached the door, opened it, stepped out, and closed the door behind him. Once outside he sprinted for the woods, and never looked back.

Luckily he was still dressed in civilian clothes. They were filthy and infested with lice, but at least he wasn't wearing prison garb. He had a chance of avoiding capture. Keeping to the woods and the back roads, Genek made his way back to Brussels. He hoped Melly would come to their meeting place at the designated time. He had no idea if she was still living in the same apartment. If she had moved and she didn't come to their rendezvous spot he did not know how he would ever find her. He prayed she hadn't been arrested too.

MELLY
VISITING BOBBY

Can you believe it? One day Genek turned up at the meeting place. I almost died of shock. I had been going there every afternoon, more to give structure to my day than because I thought there was any chance I would see my husband again. But after three months, one day there he was, leaning against a wall, hat pulled down low on his forehead, pretending to read a newspaper. I recognized him immediately. We locked eyes. Without a word I turned around and he followed me back to our apartment.

I couldn't believe he had been arrested and imprisoned and had escaped. These things just didn't happen in that time and place. People who disappeared did not come back. But Genek was a survivor, that's for sure. He was skinny and dirty but he was alive. I was very, very grateful. Look, our marriage wasn't great, but I had already lost so much. His return gave me hope again. It made me think we might come out of this ordeal alive. We might get our children back some day.

The news was mixed as we entered 1944. There was talk of an Allied invasion into Europe. We hoped and prayed that would happen soon. Everybody expected a massive land battle would have to happen to push the Nazis out of France and Belgium. In the meantime, Allied war planes were becoming more and more common, and disturbing, dropping bombs on what I guess they thought were Nazi strongholds and railways throughout Belgium, but plenty of times these bombs landed on innocent civilians. We lay in bed and listened to the booms of bombs and felt the shocks reverberate up and down our spines.

There were some instances of resistance that raised our spirits. In mid-January "Groupe G," one of the most successful Resistance cells, managed to cut electricity throughout the country. Without power, the Nazi war factories ground to halt. Of course, they resumed after a couple of days, but you see, this kind of rebellion gave our low morale a tremendous boost. Another act of resistance was the publication of fake copies of the Nazi-controlled newspaper Le Soir. The pirated paper put out strictly verboten anti-German stories. I can only imagine the wrath of the Nazi bastards when they saw those! And of course the Resistance blew up bridges and buildings and carried out assassinations. It was a time when change was starting to come to our dark continent, but slowly, and in fits and starts, two steps forward and one step back.

And of course we still couldn't trust anybody. Jacques le Gros was still on the prowl, eager to denounce his fellow Jews to the Gestapo. Everyone knew spies were everywhere. We didn't chat with our neighbors; we didn't socialize at all. You never knew who someone was working for. Maybe they were with the Resistance, but just as easily they could be informants for the Nazis. So we kept to ourselves, made no friends, and did our erratic dance from place to place, hoping to avoid detection.

Eventually I couldn't take the isolation and the loneliness anymore. I ached to see Bobby. I told Genek we had to contact the CDJ. We had to find out where Bobby was. We had to visit him.

Genek contacted the agency that had placed Bobby. I don't know how he did it, but eventually, maybe because the tide of the war was turning in our favor by then, he managed to find out where Bobby was hidden. In a convent in Banneux, about an hour outside the city. My heart was bursting with longing. I had to see my child.

Genek and I took the train out to the village. We so rarely went out together. Genek, especially since his arrest, stayed hidden indoors for weeks at a time. But he was adamant that he was coming to see Bobby with me. Genek missed our son as much as I did. And so we took the risk. We couldn't stop ourselves.

There was some commotion when we arrived at the convent. The Mother Superior was not pleased to see us. We were jeopardizing the children, we were putting the sisters in danger, blah blah. I didn't care. I had to see Bobby. We convinced her we had not been followed, that it was safe. Eventually the Mother Superior realized we were not going to be dissuaded. She told us to wait in a little alcove while one of the nuns went to fetch Bobby. I thought my heart would pound out of my chest. It was all I could do not to scream at her to hurry up.

A few minutes later a nun appeared leading a little waif by the hand. It was Bobby. He looked so pale, so thin, so scared. He didn't run to me, he didn't say a word. He was a ghost of a child. I choked back a sob, knelt and pulled him into my arms. His little body remained stiff. He didn't recognize me. His beautiful curls were shorn off. When I asked the nun why, she shrugged. Lice.

Bobby, Bobby, it's Mama, it's Mama, I said over and over again, tears pouring down my face despite my efforts not to scare him. Genek was trembling, pulling Bobby into an embrace, muttering endearments in Yiddish over and over. Bobby was silent. He looked shell-shocked.

We spent the afternoon there. Eventually Bobby gave us a small smile, his eyes brightened, and he let us hug him without the strange stiffness he had exhibited at first. He didn't talk much. I think he might have forgotten some of his Yiddish. I don't know how much he understood but we couldn't stop talking and stroking him. How do you explain to a four-year-old that you had to abandon him for a year? And that you would be leaving again.

One thing I remember. He had learned how to tie his own shoes. He was very proud. The child tugged at my hand, made me sit down beside him while he carefully worked the laces in his little boots. His huge blue eyes looked up when he was done, a spark of my Bobby's personality glinting in that thin little face. Well done, Bobby, we told him, what a big boy you are. The child smiled for the first time.

The hours flew by. A nun came in and told us it was time for us to leave. The children would be going to their dinner soon, and it was best that we not disrupt the boy any more than we already had. She stood there waiting to take my child away again. I turned my back on her, pulled Bobby close and rocked him, whispering promises and telling him I loved him over and over. But eventually I had to let him go. He looked at me with heartbreak on his wan face, but allowed the nun to lead him away. I pressed a chocolate bar into his hand and watched my little boy walk out the door. He shuffled along like a little old man. He had already had a lifetime's worth of suffering.

Genek gave the nuns some coins, begged them to buy some extra sugar for Bobby. We tried to sweeten his bleak existence the only way we could. Of course the child didn't want sugar; he wanted love, he wanted us. Genek and I wept. I thought my heart would really break. We talked about taking Bobby back with us, of course we did. But the Germans were still patrolling the streets looking for Jews. If they discovered us, if they arrested us, they would send Bobby to his death. We had to keep him safe. Leaving him again was torture, but saving his life was worth any sacrifice.

THE TIDE TURNS
BRUSSELS, 1944

The long-anticipated Allied invasion finally occurred on June 6, 1944, as American, Canadian, and British troops stormed the beaches of Normandy in northern France. They had arrived to liberate the European continent from the grip of the brutal four-year Nazi rule. D-Day, as it was called, was a massive operation. Five thousand ships, eleven thousand airplanes, and a hundred and fifty thousand soldiers launched the massive battle that would finally turn the tide of the war. The invasion was incredibly bloody. The Allies lost four thousand men on the beaches in Normandy, mowed down by German artillery and air fire. Many more were injured.

Yet they prevailed. The Allied troops advanced into France, pushing back the Germans, making their way toward Paris and toward Belgium. Despite fierce fighting, and some back-and-forth parries, the Allies managed to push the German army further and further eastward, swiftly liberating areas of France and then Belgium. On September 1, 1944, the first Allied troops crossed the Belgian frontier, and just three days later British troops arrived to liberate Brussels.

Throngs lined the streets of Brussels to welcome the Allied victors as British troops rolled into the city. Women held up babies, girls leapt into British soldiers' arms to thank them with a kiss, and thousands of ecstatic onlookers cheered and waved as their liberators drove their tanks through city streets. Long-hidden Belgian flags were unfurled and waved for the first time in four years. Ecstatic people tore down Nazi flags and ripped down German signs all over the city. Hitler was burned in effigy. Impromptu dancing broke out everywhere. The city was electric with joy, crowds of people shouting and crying and waving as they realized the hateful occupation was finally over.

Desperate Nazis, realizing their time was up, spent their final hours of occupation destroying people and evidence. They executed prisoners even as the British troops made their way into the city. Retreating Nazi soldiers set fire to the Palace of Justice in the center of Brussels, hoping to destroy documents that could be used against them by the Allies. But as the stately building burned, hundreds of Belgians organized themselves into a human chain, rescuing documents by passing them from one person to the next.

Suddenly the Nazis and their collaborators were on the run. Belgian troops, led by the intrepid Resistance, hunted for German collaborators and arrested the fleeing Nazi soldiers. In a matter of hours the hateful enemy who had dominated every aspect of life for years became prisoners of war.

On September 3–4, 1944, the remaining prisoners at Dossin Barracks at Malines found themselves suddenly free. Overnight their guards had evaporated. Some five hundred Jews who had been destined for the next transport to Auschwitz were saved. As Allied soldiers entered the camp they discovered records showing the exact number of men, women, boys, and girls who had been deported on previous transports. The dates of each train that had left had been carefully recorded by the Germans, along with how many of each age group were in that transport. In all, 25,267 innocent people had been sent from Malines to Auschwitz on twenty-eight transport trains over two years. Of them, 2,459 were children. Only a handful of the adults survived; none of the children did. Melly's Uncle Herman, Aunt Sally, and little Cousin Joachim, as well as many of Inge's friends from Lustra, were amongst those deported from Malines to Auschwitz, never to return.

Still, the war was not quite over. The Germans held on throughout the fall and winter, recapturing areas of Belgium and engaging Allied soldiers in battles. Finally, however, in February 1945, the entire country of Belgium was free.

LIBERATION
SPRING 1945

As soon as the Germans were finally pushed out of the country Genek went to collect his son from Banneux. Many of the rail lines had been destroyed in the fighting to liberate Belgium so Genek had to walk much of the way. He would have still heard the occasional drone of fighter planes as he tramped the seventy miles eastward toward the convent that had housed Bobby for the past two years. Everywhere were signs of destruction: bomb craters, burned houses, abandoned trucks. The years of war were written on the Belgian countryside.

Still, it was spring. The sun shone warmly and leaves unfurled their bright green foliage on the trees. Flowers bloomed in the fields. Birds sang from the bushes. Genek must have been reminded of the long trek he had made almost a decade earlier when he had made his way from Lvov to Belgium. As he walked he must have thought about his loved ones back in Galicia. He had not heard from them in years. Letters he had sent had received no answers. Could any of them be alive? The Nazis could not have killed everyone. There were too many people to kill, surely? They must be somewhere. Perhaps they had been sent to a ghetto, deported even. Maybe,

maybe he would find them again. He would search, he would ask everyone he met, he would go to the displaced person camps, look up the lists the Red Cross was putting together.

Eventually the village came into view. Genek quickened his pace. He was going to get Bobby. He was going to bring his precious son home. The Nazi mumzers had taken a lot from him, but his most darling jewel of a son was safe. He and Melly had missed years of their son's childhood; they would never get that back. But if the child survived the war that was all that mattered.

Genek entered the convent and met with the Mother Superior. She remembered him from the time he and Melly had come to visit Bobby. She greeted him warmly, obviously surprised and pleased that he was still alive. Yes, she told him, your son is still here and he is well. We will fetch him for you.

And so once again Genek waited in the alcove while a nun went to collect little Bobby. As he came into view Genek noticed he had grown. His baby face had changed. He was painfully thin. As he knelt before him he saw some white hairs growing on Bobby's temples. How could a five-year-old child have white hair? Genek enveloped Bobby in his arms.

As before, at first Bobby's body remained stiff and unyielding as Genek hugged him and spoke to him in Yiddish. He didn't answer. Then the child brought his face close to his father's neck and inhaled a few times. Suddenly Bobby smiled. So much time had gone by that he barely remembered his father's face. But his scent. That triggered a cascade of memories. Bobby knew this man, and knew the man loved him. He clung to Genek and Genek clung to him, tears running down both their faces.

Genek wasted no time on niceties at the convent. He wanted to bring Bobby home. Lifting the child onto his shoulders, he quickly departed and started the long walk back through the Belgian countryside, heading toward Brussels. Bobby weighed so little, he barely slowed Genek's stride as he retraced his steps. As he walked he spoke to Bobby in Yiddish, telling him how much he had missed him, how happy he was to be bringing him back, how excited Mama would be to see him. Mein tachschit, Bobby, he told the child, you are my jewel.

Bobby listened to the man's voice, understanding little. He had barely spoken for the past two years. He had rarely been outside. Now he was moving, carried on the strong shoulders of this man, Papa, while an avalanche of sensations bombarded his sensory-deprived brain. The sun was very bright. And warm. There were trees and flowers and houses, sounds and smells. There was a breeze blowing on his face. Overwhelmed, Bobby dozed as Genek walked.

Suddenly the drone of an approaching airplane made Genek jump. It was a fighter plane, flying low and fast. In a flash Genek lifted Bobby off his shoulders, tossed him onto the ground and threw his body over that of his little son. Folding his hands over his head he remained prone until the plane was gone. Bobby's little body shook with fright.

It's alright, Bobby, it's alright, he told him. I'm here. You're safe. I will protect you. Come on, let's get going. Genek lifted Bobby back onto his shoulders and continued walking.

Eventually they came to a main road. Genek, tired from the long walk to Banneux and back, decided that walking a straight route on a real road was better than meandering along country paths, and the best way to get home quickly. The only trouble was, soldiers used these roads too. Genek hoped that they would get to Brussels without incident, and if they were passed by convoys he hoped the soldiers would be friendly ones.

Sure enough, after a couple of hours a convoy of trucks approached from behind them, heading, it seemed, toward Brussels as they were. As they neared, Genek could see they were American soldiers. He waved. One of the trucks pulled to a stop and a group of smiling American G.I.s motioned for Genek and Bobby to hop up onto the back of the truck.

Hey buddy, need a lift? one of them called. Give me your little boy, and climb on up!

Genek passed Bobby up to the American soldiers, who hoisted him aboard. For a panicky moment Bobby thought his father was abandoning him again. He cried out. But Genek climbed in right behind him. Wearily he sat down and thanked the G.I.s for picking them up. The soldiers were young and fit and very friendly. They looked so different from the gaunt and gray Europeans Genek was used to seeing.

Not a problem, buddy, one said. Where ya headed? Brussels? We are too! And with that the truck rumbled on with its two additional passengers, little Bobby staring in awe at the countryside now whizzing by at an astonishing speed. One of the American soldiers was Jewish. He and Genek excitedly struck up a conversation in Yiddish, Genek explaining what he was doing out on the road with his child. Bobby watched his father, watched the soldiers, wondered if he was dreaming.

The Americans had chocolate. Seeing the skinny little child, they dug into their supply and gave Bobby as much candy as they could find. He had not had sweets in so long that Bobby crammed the chocolates into his mouth as fast as the G.I.s produced it. Bobby looked at the faces of these new men. They spoke some language he had never heard before; he couldn't understand what they said. And one of them had a chocolate-colored face. He had never seen a man that color before. Maybe he had eaten too much chocolate? But they were nice. They smiled and laughed and looked kind and they gave him candy. Papa seemed relaxed with them. What an amazing day this was.

And so Bobby arrived back home just in time for his fifth birthday. His father carried him up the stairs to their apartment at 32 Rue des Ménapiens. His arrival was marred by his getting violently sick from all the chocolate he had eaten on the American truck, a stomach-churning combination with the travel and excitement of the day. So it was not exactly the joyous celebration Melly had envisioned. But he soon recovered. His parents were ecstatic to have him home. Except for a couple of months in the spring of 1943, he had been separated from his family for two and a half years, half of his young life.

Now it was time to get Irene back.

MELLY
IRENE

It was the spring of 1945. The war was over. We had survived against all odds. My family reunited in Brussels. My mother returned to the city, having successfully hidden up north with her employers. Nathan was back as well; he had left Banneux and walked back to Brussels and showed up at Inge's apartment one day. And Inge, while still sickly since her illness, had made it too. We had Bobby back. As soon as we got my beautiful baby girl back my joy would be complete, and our family could move on from the horrors of the past few years.

Having Bobby home was wonderful. He was darling. His reserve slowly dissipated and he became chatty, inquisitive. I loved him as I had never loved anyone, fiercely and fully, and he reciprocated my affection. Despite the years of separation we were as close as could be. He did have nightmares sometimes, but when I went into his room he let me hold him and soothe him. I couldn't wait to get Irene back too and make our family whole again. We had survived. We would be together again. It seemed like a dream.

We asked Nathan to bring us to Namur to show us the house where Irene had been hidden. We decided to go on a Sunday, hoping to catch the people when they were likely to be home. It didn't occur to me that there would be a problem. Sure, the family might have grown fond of the child, and maybe our arrival would be a surprise, but after all, we were the parents. I expected we would scoop up our child, thank the people who had guarded her, and return to Brussels as a united family at last. Getting Bobby back had been easy, I didn't think getting Irene back would be any different.

Bobby came with us, of course. He didn't remember having met Irene when she was a newborn. He didn't understand who she was or how she fit into the family. She's our daughter, your sister, I told him. What's a sister? he kept asking me. Mama, what's a sister? I laughed. You'll see, Bobby, she's a little girl who will love you very much. I smoothed back his curls, noticing, as I always did, the scattering of white hairs on his little head.

We took the train to Namur: Genek and I, Bobby, and Nathan. Nathan reminisced about the experience of following baby Irene two years earlier, how he had watched the priest accept the child, and then observed him bring her to a home and give her to a middle-aged couple. I found myself wondering who they were. A small niggle of worry rose in my throat, but I pushed it away. We had managed to get Bobby back, and we would now get Irene.

Nathan led us through the streets of Namur until we arrived at a tidy little cottage. I saw a child's toy, a baby doll stroller, in the front yard, a rag doll propped up within it. Genek rang the doorbell. A kindly-looking woman answered the door, smoothing her hands on her apron. She greeted us in French, explained they were just finishing Sunday dinner. Could she help us? Genek looked nervous, and I found my heart beating furiously in my chest. We are Genek and Melly Bottner, Madame, he told her. I believe our little daughter has been living here?

The woman shook her head, looking puzzled. I think you may be at the wrong house, she said. Just then a younger man appeared behind her. He wore the white collar of a priest. What is it, Mama? he asked. When we explained who we were the priest looked aghast. He put a hand on the older woman's shoulder. Let them in, Mama, he said. He invited us all into the house. We sat on the sofa and made introductions.

It was then that I caught a glimpse of my daughter. I hadn't seen her since she was three months old. Now she was over two, a pudgy adorable little thing with wild brown curls. It was obvious she had not been deprived of food. She toddled over to Madame Bouchat – I had just found out her name – and the woman picked her up and set her on her hip. Irene hid her face in the woman's shoulder. My heart beat even harder. I swallowed.

Hello, darling Irene, I tried.

The child would not take her face out of Madame's neck.

Nathan started talking then. He explained how he had trailed the baby when she was picked up and brought to Namur. He told the priest he had watched him receive the child and bring her here, to the house we had just learned was that of his parents. Nathan explained that we were Jewish, we had given up our child because we were in grave danger of arrest and deportation. But we had survived and now we were here to bring our child home.

The Bouchats stared at us, shaking their heads. They had an animated conversation with the priest, who turned out to be their son. The priest hung his head and explained that, yes, the little one was a hidden Jewish child. She had not been abandoned on the church steps. He had in fact received her from contacts in the Resistance who were hiding Jewish children. He kept apologizing to them.

Madame clung to Irene and started crying. No, no, this can't be, she kept saying. The older Monsieur too became very agitated. Perhaps you are mistaken, he said. Why do you think this particular child is yours? She has been with us since infancy.

It was then that we mentioned the scar, the surgical mark we had made on Irene's right thigh. I thanked God that we had had the foresight to mark our baby. Because otherwise there really would have been no proof that she was ours.

Irene, reacting perhaps to the agitation in the house, started crying. She had a loud and piercing cry. I got up and walked over to Madame, hoping to take Irene into my own arms to soothe her. Irene went crazy, screaming, kicking, and yelling Mama, Mama! as she clung to Madame's neck. She would have nothing to do with me. She didn't know me. To her I was a stranger.

I am your mama, I told her. But the child kept crying and pushing me away.

Madame carried her into the other room, both of them weeping and clinging to each other. Monsieur and Father Bouchat looked stunned as Genek tried to thank them for everything they had done to care for our baby.

But she is our child, Monsieur protested. We love her. We adopted her, we are raising her. Tears appeared in the older man's eyes. Bobby clutched my hand and watched this scene with huge eyes. I felt his little body trembling as voices were raised and emotions ran higher and higher.

Genek eventually had had enough. He was not a patient man. He had a temper.

Listen, he said, this situation is getting worse by the minute. We are Irene's parents. I am sorry you thought you could keep her. You can't. We are taking her home with us now.

He walked into the room where Madame was sitting with Irene nestled in her arms, and reached for the child. Both Madame and Irene started wailing. Irene kicked and clawed like a wild animal. Genek had to wrestle her out of Madame's arms.

For a moment I remembered when I had to give up little Bobby when he was just two years old, and my heart went out to the woman. But then I thought, no. This woman has her own children. She has no right to covet this child of mine. I am the victim here. I am the one whose child was taken from me. My heart hardened again.

The Bouchats pleaded with us to wait, to give them time to get used to the idea, to let the child get to know us before we did anything rash. But Genek was adamant now. We would not be repeating this scene, he told them. While we were very grateful that they had cared for our girl, and sorry that they were hurt, it was time to go.

Carrying the hysterical toddler, he marched out of the house, little Bobby and I following. The last image I had of Madame and Monsieur Bouchat was of the two of them standing with their arms around each other, crying. Nathan stayed back to try to make amends, but there was little he could say, and he soon caught up with us as we made our way back toward the train station.

Irene did not stop crying and screaming the entire way back to Brussels. By the time we got home I half wished we hadn't gone to get her. My head was killing me. She wouldn't let me near her. Eventually, out of sheer exhaustion, she fell asleep on the sofa. But the minute she woke up it was back to wailing and calling for her mama. And she didn't mean me.

Genek tried to console me. Give it a little time, Melly, he told me. She's a little child. She isn't trying to be bad. She's scared. But he too became impatient when Irene kept crying and carrying on day in and day out. When he couldn't take the screaming any more Genek went out. I was left to deal with Irene. Eventually I tucked her into bed with Bobby. That seemed to quiet her down. She snuggled into her brother, put her thumb in her mouth, and fell asleep.

And you know, that became a pattern. Irene rejected me, wouldn't let me mother her. And I, young and foolish and distraught, allowed a terrible distance to form between us. I stopped trying to comfort her when she cried; I put her into bed with Bobby instead. I stopped trying to win her over. I lavished my maternal affection on the child who loved me back, and I kept away from the one who seemed to hate me.

Genek was a little more understanding with Irene's response to us. But he too was an emotional wreck after the war. The strain of hiding, of losing his family, of separating from our children, had damaged him as well. He was impatient, angry. Sure, he still had his sense of humor – Genek was always one for a laugh – but when Irene screamed and cried for hours he lost his temper with her. Poor child. The only one she bonded with was Bobby.

Looking back, I know I made a terrible mistake. I rejected my own child, the only daughter I would ever have. She was a baby. She couldn't help her reaction. She was traumatized, plucked from the only family she had ever known by strangers and brought to live in a house where she knew no-one, didn't even speak the language. She was in terrible pain. But I could deal with only so much suffering. Irene's mourning of her Namur family, her rejection of me and Genek, felt like she was spitting in the face of the sorrow we had gone through to keep her alive. I felt only anger toward her.

I should have understood. But I'm ashamed to say I didn't. I too was traumatized. I was twenty-three years old, but felt eighty-three. I had been through so much tsures in my own life that it had left me bitter. My emotional state was brittle and fragile, sadly lacking in the wisdom I needed to parent my estranged child. For two long and lonely years I had pined for my darling little girl, envisioning the moment she would be back in my arms. Instead I found myself with a sullen screaming brat who rejected me.

Foolish, foolish woman that I was, I rejected her in turn. We never managed to bridge the yawning distance those terrible first years apart had created. Our emotional estrangement remained even as Irene grew older, stopped screaming for her other mama. I did not shower her with affection as I did Bobby. I kept her at arm's length. My daughter never felt loved in my home. I failed her. For Irene too it was a schver bitter leiben.

It wasn't until I was on my deathbed that I apologized to her.

AFTER LIBERATION

When he returned to Brussels, Nathan searched for and found his sister Inge. Melly and Genek and their children were now reunited and living together in Brussels too. But they all missed and worried about their mother. Gertrude had been out of the city for years, living in a small village up north by the Dutch border together with the couple who had employed her as a housekeeper during the war. The three siblings had not seen their mother in a long time. There had been little communication. Had anything happened to Gertrude? Was she alright? Until they knew for sure she was alive and well, they worried. By now they surmised their father was dead. Reports were trickling in of the evacuation of the inmates of Apeldoornse Bos to Auschwitz.

Nathan decided to look for his mother. Trains were not running up to the north of Belgium yet; that part of the country was still occupied by the Germans. Nathan asked some English soldiers on the street about going up to the village where he believed his mother was living. Don't do it, they replied, the area is still full of German soldiers, it's too dangerous.

But Nathan was undeterred. He got hold of an old bicycle and, smiling at his sisters' pleas to be careful, started off on the bike to find the village. He was seventeen years old, and had been taking care of himself for years by then. A bike ride in the countryside would not scare him, German soldiers or no.

Eventually Nathan did find the village and had a tearful reunion with his mother Gertrude. She had indeed survived the war by hiding with her employers and working as a housekeeper. Interestingly, the area seemed devoid of Germans. After spending a few days with Gertrude, Nathan cycled back to Brussels, happily relaying the news to his sisters that their mother was indeed fine. He also informed the English soldiers that the north of Belgium no longer seemed to be occupied.

Nevertheless, it took seven additional weeks for the Allies to deem the north of the country liberated. At that time Gertrude returned from the village and was reunited with her children in Brussels. She, Inge, and Nathan lived together in one apartment, and Melly, Genek, and their small children, Bobby and Irene, lived in another. After years of occupation, terror, hiding, and deprivation, it was time to start living again.

Belgium, like the rest of Europe, was awakening after five years of despair. Shops were again open, cafes were full, people were strolling the streets and chatting in parks. Movie theaters thrived. Nathan saw his first Disney movie. He went to the opera.

For a few months Nathan worked as an apprentice in the diamond industry in Antwerp. He traveled from Brussels to Antwerp daily by train, making the once danger-fraught journey in under half an hour. The country was once again navigable. His job was to learn the diamond-cutting business from his Uncle Shlomo, Gertrude's youngest brother, who had somehow also survived the Holocaust.

But the diamond business didn't interest Nathan. He was looking for a purpose, for meaning in his life. In the wake of the war,

Zionist groups, intent on creating a Jewish state in Palestine, were thriving among Jewish survivors. Nathan joined a youth movement called Hashomer Hatza'ir.

This movement had originated in Eastern Europe after World War One. Its mission was the creation of a Socialist Jewish homeland. Between the world wars the group had already founded several kibbutzim in Palestine, established by members who had emigrated from Europe. By 1939 the organization had seventy thousand members worldwide. During the war Hashomer Hatza'ir was involved in resisting the Nazis, aiding in the Warsaw Ghetto Uprising, and in rescue missions for Jews in Lithuania, Slovakia, and Hungary. Many of its members had been captured and executed during World War Two.

Hashomer Hatza'ir was recruiting young Jewish survivors in Europe after the war, and in this organization Nathan found the purpose he was looking for. Horrified by the Holocaust, by watching friends and family shamed, humiliated, robbed, imprisoned, beaten, and killed, Nathan, like many Jews, vowed "never again." The Brussels chapter of the Zionist group, consisting of about a dozen teenage boys and girls, ushered friendship and meaning into his life. He agreed wholeheartedly with the Zionist vision of a Jewish homeland. He wanted to devote his life to this cause; he started thinking about emigrating.

Gertrude too was moving on with her life. Soon after returning to Brussels she met another survivor, a German Jew named Shlomo Kliegsberg. She knew her husband Leopold had died at Auschwitz. And in any case, she had not lived with him in almost a decade. Still in the middle of her life, her children grown or almost grown, she, like the rest of Europe, turned her eyes to the future. A year after returning to Brussels Gertrude married Shlomo Kliegsberg, a kind and friendly man who brought joy back into her lonely life.

Inge also found love. At the end of the war she met a soldier named Hans Kerpen. Hans, handsome, charming, and kind, was serving in the British army. He belonged to the Jewish Brigade from Palestine. His family had fled from Austria, establishing themselves in Palestine before the war. As part of the British Empire, Palestine supplied soldiers to serve in the war effort. Hans was stationed in Brussels as a British soldier.

The two started dating. Gertrude, uncomfortable with her young daughter going off with a man unsupervised, enlisted little Bobby to act as chaperone when they went out. To keep Bobby busy, Inge and Hans often took the child to swimming pools. Bobby would happily go for a swim, while the young adults drank coffee in the pool's cafe. In this way they courted. Sometimes they bought Bobby ice cream. They wanted him to enjoy these outings so that they could continue seeing each other.

Inge, smitten with the handsome young man, listened wide-eyed as the young Jewish soldier regaled her with tales of his homeland, still under British occupation, but hopefully soon to become an independent Jewish state. Before he was shipped back out, he begged Inge to join him in Eretz Israel. The two young people seemed to recognize each other as kindred spirits. Each one saw the kindness and love they had in their own soul reflected in the other's eyes.

Once her mother remarried, Inge found herself the lost middle child once again. With Gertrude now in a new marriage, Melly busy with her own husband and children, and Nathan involved in Hashomer Hatza'ir, Inge missed Hans terribly. She wanted to build a life with him, in a new place, away from the horrors of Europe. At the end of 1946 she left for Palestine on an illegal ship bound for the port of Haifa. She was twenty-one years old.

Traveling on illegal ships from Europe to Palestine was incredibly dangerous. The ships were battle-weary and in poor repair.

Conditions on board were horrible, with little shelter, overcrowding, and insufficient food and water. Several ships foundered and sank after colliding on rocks or running into mines. Often, they were pursued by British warships intent on intercepting them. These interceptions sometimes turned violent. Nevertheless, thousands of desperate people boarded these ships, eager to flee from the continent.

Jewish entry into Palestine was severely restricted at this time. Even after the destruction of two-thirds of Europe's Jewish population in the Holocaust, Britain, bowing to Arab pressure, was turning away or imprisoning Jews attempting to enter Palestine. When Inge's ship arrived in Haifa, Inge and the other Jewish Holocaust survivors from Europe were brought to a detention camp in Atlit, just south of the port of Haifa, by the British authorities. Luckily she was only detained there briefly.

In early 1947 she was released from Atlit and reunited with her beau. She and Hans, who had by now left the British army, were married in Palestine. Inge was warmly welcomed into Hans's family. Inge became the first of her family to escape Europe and establish a life in what would soon be the land of Israel.

Back in Brussels, Nathan continued his involvement with Hashomer Hatza'ir. Nathan and his friends, the other young members of this group, all wanted to get into Palestine and establish a Jewish state. Nathan's new stepfather Shlomo helped the youth group contact an organization that was clandestinely smuggling Jews into Palestine. This group was called Aliyah Bet.

Bet is the second letter of the Hebrew alphabet. Aliyah Bet referred to getting Jews who were not legally allowed entry by the British (due to restrictive quotas) into the country. Aliyah Aleph, aleph being the first letter of the Hebrew alphabet, referred to legal immigration within the quotas.

Many of the Jewish survivors of the Holocaust, most of whom had been in the killing camps, were now destitute, homeless, and living in wretched conditions. Having survived against unbelievable odds, they now found themselves living in displaced persons camps, many inside Germany, as they had nowhere else to go. The object of the Aliyah Bet was to transport as many of these Jewish survivors as possible into Palestine, ignoring the British quotas, and trying to evade the British navy that stood in the way.

In March 1947 Nathan's chapter of Hashomer Hatza'ir found itself on the move, beginning its journey to Palestine. On instruction from members of the Aliyah Bet, the group left Brussels and made their way to a chateau in the south of Belgium in a town called Boneff. Here other young Jews, survivors from all over Europe, came together to organize for emigration. They only stayed here for a few days, but it turned out to be an extremely important few days for Nathan.

One evening at Chateau Boneff, Nathan and another boy, his cousin Jackie, found themselves at a ping-pong table where two pretty girls were playing a match. Soon they joined the girls and the four young people continued the game. One of the girls, a tiny young beauty with curling brown hair and blue eyes, was Regina Hershkowitz. Nathan learned that Regina and her sister Hermine had survived Auschwitz and Bergen-Belsen. Later Regina would change her name to Shoshana; Hermine would become Shula. Little did Nathan know how important Regina/Shoshana would become in his life.

After a couple of days the young people moved on to the French town of Sète, near Marseilles. After a few more days in Sète, they were brought into the harbor where they saw the ship that was to carry them to Palestine. The Theodor Hertzl was a forty-year-old rust bucket salvaged from the U.S. and roughly refurbished in France by the Aliyah Bet. She had a coal-fueled engine and could mount a maximum speed of eight knots.

On April 2, 1947, the Theodor Hertzl was loaded with 2,641 young Jewish passengers and she set sail under a Spanish crew with a young Jewish commander named Mordechai (or Mecca) Limon, a member of the Haganah who would eventually become the Commander of the Navy in the State of Israel. The boat was terribly crowded. There were no cabins. The passengers slept on wooden shelves built into the hold, with only about twenty-five inches' clearance between them.

From the start the voyage was problematic. The ship was supposed to pick up additional Jewish refugees in Italy and Turkey, but both of these rendezvous were abandoned due to miscommunication. The vessel ran into a minefield as she approached Egypt. There was little food and water, and the boat was terribly crowded. But the passengers were tough young survivors, and they cared little about comfort. Their goal was to escape Europe and get to their ancestral homeland.

Nathan refused to sleep on the cramped wooden shelves. He made his way onto the deck, taking his chances with the elements rather than the claustrophobic hold. Regina/Shoshana slept down below.

After eleven days at sea, on April 13, as they neared Palestine, the passengers saw three British warships steaming toward them. These ships easily caught and surrounded the Theodor Hertzl. One British ship rammed into the stern and British sailors jumped aboard the smaller vessel.

When the British boarded the Theodor Hertzl the Jewish young people resisted. A hand-to-hand battle commenced. Jewish teenagers, weaponless, attacked the British sailors with vegetable crates. They tossed one British sailor overboard. The British, shocked at the resistance, opened fire. Three young Jewish refugees were killed and twenty-seven were injured before the Theodor Hertzl was subdued. The boat was damaged during the fight, and had to be towed into the harbor at Haifa.

Desperate Jewish refugees found themselves literally on the shores of the land they had dreamed about, but forbidden from entering. As the dead and wounded were carried off the ship, the rest of the passengers were informed by the British that they were to be transferred to Cyprus for internment in camps for illegal immigrants. The heartbroken passengers unfurled a sign that they hung over the side of the boat. It read, in English, "The Germans destroyed our families and homes, don't you destroy our hopes."

From the crowded deck Nathan watched the British ship Ocean Vigour and two other large British ships waiting to take them away. One by one the Jewish refugees were lead off the Theodor Hertzl by two British sailors, and ushered up the wooden gangplanks and onto the waiting British vessels. There was no escape.

Soon they set sail again, watching the shores of Palestine again fade away as they steamed north toward the island of Cyprus. They had come so far and gotten so close, only to be rebuffed, refused refuge, once again. On board were over 2,400 young people who had come of age in a time of horror, most of whom had lost their families, all of whom had lost their homes, and who were destitute and desperate. Even after traveling across the European continent and across the Mediterranean, even as they arrived on the shores of their intended homeland, they were still unable to find a place to call home. Nobody wanted them. There would be no happy ending. Not yet.

Nathan and the other refugees who had been aboard the Theodor Hertzl were shipped to Cyprus, where they were individually off-loaded and "processed." Each refugee was registered and sprayed with DDT to delouse him, and then assigned a barrack in the British prison camp.

Nathan was assigned to Camp 68, a tent camp in the desert, surrounded by barbed wire. This camp was in the location known as the "winter camps" in Dekhelia, near Larnaca. Another site about fifty miles away near the city of Famagusta housed what were called the "summer camps." Only two crude buildings existed in Camp 68, one for cooking and dining, and the other for tending to the sick. The thousands of people living in the camp were housed in tents erected in close proximity in straight lines, forming a compound. Nearby were other camps: Camp 64 was beside them, and across the street were Camps 65, 66, and 67. By the time Nathan left the camp twenty-two months later, two more, Camp 70 and 80, had sprung up.

Every month 750 certificates were issued by the British allowing for that many Jewish prisoners to leave Cyprus and legally emigrate to Palestine. The remaining tens of thousands of people languished in Cyprus, awaiting their turn.

Nathan, ever resourceful and uncowed by the incarceration, made the most of the situation. He had learned to speak English during that year he had spent living in London with his father. Thus he was able to communicate with the British guards – which was very unusual among the refugees. The guards decided to give Nathan a job. Every day he was tasked with collecting food for the camp. He drove a truck out of the gate and to another site where the British stored food. Nathan was accompanied by a British soldier named Johnny, who came along to guard the process. Nathan loaded the truck with food supplies daily and then drove the truck back to Camp 68, bringing the food to the kitchen/dining building where it was unloaded and then prepared into meals by other prisoners. Thus Nathan spent the first few months of his Cyprus incarceration.

After many months, as more Jews were slowly taken out of the Cyprus camps and brought to Israel, Nathan and his group were able to relocate from the tents to the newly vacated and more desirable tin barracks. Conditions there were only marginally better, however, with no electricity or running water, and ongoing problems with extremes of ambient temperature.

The good part of the move to new quarters, however, was that Nathan was reunited with the pretty girl named Regina. The two formed a strong connection. Regina was a seventeen-year-old orphan. She was highly traumatized and nervous. Nathan found himself strongly drawn to the girl, wanting to protect her and to help her heal. In turn, Nathan's steady presence gave her the strength to eventually tell him her story. The two spent long hours walking around the camp, holding hands and sharing the ways in which they had survived the war. Regina had decided to change her name. From now on she would be called Shoshana. Like many survivors, she happily shed her European name, choosing a new one to symbolize her symbolic rebirth as a free person.

Regina was born in a town called Tornalla, Slovakia, close to the Hungarian border. Hers was a large family of eight children, who lived together with their mother and father. When she was a small child the area was taken over by the Hungarians. So Regina grew up speaking Hungarian. Because Hungary was part of the Austrian-Hungarian Empire, the Jews of this country were relatively protected until later in the war. It wasn't until 1944 that Hitler got around to annihilating the Hungarian Jewish population. But in 1944 life screeched to a halt. Regina's two eldest brothers were sent to a work camp. The rest of the family was shipped in cattle cars to Auschwitz.

How on earth did you survive? asked Nathan.

I had three angels, she told him. Three angels who saved my life.

Nathan wrapped his arm around the girl's thin frame and, pulling her close, murmured, tell me.

When Regina and her family got to Auschwitz, they stumbled off the train, completely disoriented from the journey in the dark, cramped, and airless compartment. They tried to stay together, but guards were screaming and there was a lot of confusion and fear. Regina's sister Hermine, though, was with her. They held hands.

They were herded along, through the gates of the camp, and told to line up. As they were waiting in line, a Polish man approached them. He was the skinniest man Regina had ever seen, dressed in striped rags, and he was her first angel.

In Yiddish he asked them how old they were. Fifteen and sixteen, they replied. No, he said. You are now eighteen and nineteen. Remember. It's important. Then he disappeared.

They watched as the people in front of them got toward the front of the line where a couple of S.S. officers were stationed. Some of the people from their train were sent in one direction, most in another. They didn't know what it meant. When they got to the front, trembling, still holding hands, the officers asked their ages. They said eighteen and nineteen. The S.S. officer looked them up and down, then nodded and indicated that they should step to the right. They watched as their mother and little sister and baby brother were motioned to the left.

Later they understood. Going to the right meant they would be admitted to Auschwitz. Going to the left meant straight to the gas chamber. They never saw their mother, sister, or brother again. Hermine and Regina were tattooed with numbers on their arms. And they came into the living hell that was Auschwitz.

Shoshana took a few deep breaths. She started to cry. Nathan held her, whispered comforting words in her ear. Eventually she found the strength to resume her story.

In exchange for the privilege of living, they had to work for the Nazis.

Shoshana would not tell Nathan all of it. It was too awful. But she did tell him about when she met her second angel.

Every day they had to march to the work site. It was far and it was very cold. They had no coats, their feet were frozen in the snow, they were shivering, starving. Every day prisoners gave up. All you had to do was stop, fall down in the snow, and the guards would shoot you. And just like that it could be over. Regina thought about it all the time.

But there was one German guard who sang while they were marching. Over and over he sang this German song – it was something like "all things come to an end, after every December there comes May." Regina listened to the words and they gave her strength. They brought her hope. His singing saved her life for the second time. Because of him she kept marching. She didn't lie down in the snow. Yes, a German soldier was her second angel.

The war was going badly for the Germans but, even as they realized they were going to lose, they intensified their efforts to make the world free of Jews, cleansed of Jews. Judenrein. This was the most important thing for them.

Eventually they decided to move the prisoners from Auschwitz to Bergen-Belsen. Naturally the camp inmates had to march. This was really a death march. By now they were so emaciated and weak that people were dropping left and right. But Hermine and Regina were still together, thank God. They had each other. Most people were completely alone. Anyway, they marched for a very long time. Days. Eventually Hermine couldn't do it anymore. I'm going to stop, she told Regina. Her sister begged her not to, but Hermine had no more strength. She lay down in the snow.

And here, Regina said, her third angel appeared. Because the guards didn't shoot Hermine. Perhaps they thought she was already dead, because they just picked her up and tossed her onto the truck that was carrying the corpses of all the other people who had died or been killed during the march. Regina also thought she was dead, of course. She was in a very bad state of mind. But a miracle happened. When they arrived at Bergen-Belsen, Hermine was again with Regina. She told her sister that when she lay on that truck full of corpses she found she didn't want to die. So she jumped off and she started walking again. So they were together when they entered Bergen-Belsen. And they lived in that hell for some time.

The British came one day and liberated the camp. And they survived. Three angels saved them.

The British soldiers helped the prisoners when they liberated the camp. They gave them sips of water; they didn't let them eat too much right away. You know, when you have been starving you have to start eating again very slowly. The British gave them a ride to Budapest. But Hermine got very sick. She and Regina were in the hospital for a while, but they recovered.

And the rest of your family? What happened to them? asked Nathan after a while.

Regina's father had died of typhus. He actually survived until the camp was liberated, but he died anyway, before he could leave. After the war the sisters found that three of their brothers had survived. So compared to most people they were lucky. Out of ten of them, five survived.

But Hermine and Regina couldn't stay in Europe after all that had happened. They wanted to go to Palestine, to live in a new place where no-one would try to kill them for being Jews. So they joined Hashomer Hatza'ir.

Shoshana sighed and snuggled closer into Nathan's lean body.

And you know the rest of the story.

The two teenagers gazed into each other's blue eyes. Was the fluke of having been born with blue eyes the reason they were now alive and not dead like so many others? Neither expressed this grim thought. They simply clung to each other, each knowing that they had found the person they would be with for the rest of their lives.

NATHAN'S FREEDOM
CYPRUS AND PALESTINE, 1947–1949

A few months into his imprisonment, Nathan managed to buy a small electric Philips radio during one of his trips outside the camp, and to smuggle it back when he returned to his barrack. The magnitude of this boon was unimaginable. The prisoners had no access to newspapers, and were completely cut off from what was happening in the world. Crucially, they were unaware of progress being made toward the creation of the State of Israel.

There was a problem, however. The radio ran only on electricity, not on batteries. And there was no electricity in the barracks. Nathan recruited a couple of friends and the boys set themselves to the task of covertly bringing electricity in. First they snipped pieces of barbed wire from the perimeter fence that enclosed the camp. Next they soaked the wire in petrol for a few days. They carefully removed the barbs, and then spliced the lengths of wire together to form long cables. The process was slow but eventually they had enough wire to reach the infirmary, where there was a source of electric current. Somehow they managed to connect the wires. They created makeshift switches out of tin cans. Eventually they were able to connect the little radio to a source of current and to hear the news.

With the radio functioning they could finally learn what was going on in the world. On November 29, 1947, Nathan listened to the live radio broadcast as the United Nations voted about partitioning Palestine to create a Jewish state. When the required two-thirds majority was finally gained, he raced out of the barrack and called out the miraculous news to the other young Jewish detainees. A spontaneous celebration broke out. The dream was becoming a reality. For the first time Jews would have their own country, where they would be free. No more antisemitic hatred, no more anti-Jewish legislature, no more pogroms, no more concentration camps, no more Nazi atrocities, no more genocide.

The camp became a party, as elated young people joined hands and broke out into Hebrew songs. Around and around they danced, stamping feet, laughing, and throwing their arms around each other. They had survived, and now perhaps they would thrive.

Despite this incredible victory, the imprisonment went on. The British were still in charge, and their immigration laws were still in place. Even after the young people listened to David Ben-Gurion declare the formation of the autonomous State of Israel on May 14, 1948, the detainees on Cyprus were not released. Fighting was going on 300 miles away between the Arabs, the Jews, and the withdrawing British. War was not yet over.

The Jews of Palestine, eventually Israel, had not forgotten about the prisoners in Cyprus, however. Throughout the duration of the Cyprus prison camps, emissaries had come to visit, give hope, provide updates, and even train and recruit young people for the Haganah, the organization that would eventually become the Israeli army.

The mood of the camp lifted. Cultural life blossomed, despite the abysmal living conditions. The Jewish prisoners organized choirs, and put on theatrical performances. Many of the young Jews affiliated themselves with kibbutzim, well before they ever stepped foot inside Israel, and spent many hours in meetings, organizing details of their intended communities.

The kibbutz was an idea the Zionist groups had promulgated even back in the Diaspora. The idea was a socialist one: the formation of communities where members shared everything – housing, work, governance, costs, and profits. Most were agricultural communities. Some actual kibbutzim were already flourishing in the territory of the newly minted Israel, and had been for decades. Other kibbutzim were still in the planning stages. But members were organizing and getting ready for the time they could plant their first crop and build their first house. When they hit the ground in Israel they would be ready.

The young Jewish Holocaust survivors embraced the ideal of the kibbutz. After the horrors of Europe, the concept of these idyllic communities of fellow Jews resonated strongly. Not all of them would actually live in kibbutzim when they finally got to Israel. But the philosophy of community-based living would influence them all.

Ever so slowly, 750 people per month, the prisoners were released from the prison camps and shipped out of Cyprus into Israel. The rule was "first in, first out." But the reality was that young men of fighting age were the last to be freed. The British knew these youth, once released, would surely be recruited by the Israeli Haganah and would soon be involved in the civil war that was raging all over the tiny country. So they detained the young people in Cyprus as long as possible. Nathan, who had entered the camps in early 1947, languished there until January 1949.

There were additional roadblocks. In 1947 the refugee ship Exodus was detained by the British as she approached Haifa. A violent skirmish broke out, with many dead and wounded. This time, instead of sending the refugees to Cyprus as usual, the irate British decided to return the Holocaust survivors to Europe. The incident garnered a lot of international press and well-deserved outrage. The Exodus eventually went all the way back to Germany with her load of traumatized people, depositing them back in the country that had vowed to annihilate them from the earth.

After that event, Golda Meir, then acting head of the Jewish Agency's Political Department, came to Cyprus to speak to the Jewish detainees. Her mission was twofold. She asked the prisoners in Cyprus to allow some of the precious entry visas to be used for the people who would otherwise be returned to Europe, such as the Exodus's passengers. She also begged for babies who were sick with typhus inside the Cyprus camps to be allowed to jump the queue so they could be transported immediately to Palestine, where Jewish hospitals waited to care for them. Essentially she was asking Holocaust survivors from Europe who had already been imprisoned for months in Cyprus to accept a further delay in their release on altruistic grounds. It was a tough sell.

But the prisoners agreed. They preferred to stay in prison for a few more months than to see Jewish babies die of disease. They had seen enough children die. The next shipment of freed prisoners was called the "baby transport." It consisted of sick infants and their parents, allowed to jump the queue and get to Palestine right away.

But eventually Nathan's turn came. On January 25, 1949, he boarded the ship Galilah, leaving Cyprus behind him forever, setting his gaze toward Haifa, Israel. Beside him was the beautiful girl he had met back in Belgium and with whom he had bonded during their years of captivity in Cyprus. Her name was now Shoshana. Nathan had twin goals: to reunite with his family, and to marry Shoshana as soon as possible.

He managed both. His mother and sisters had managed to get to Israel before him, and all were overjoyed to have their boy Nathan free and finally in Israel. Theirs was a joyous reunion. And only three weeks later, on February 12, 1949, Nathan and Shoshana were married.

MELLY
BRUSSELS AND PALESTINE, 1945–1949

After the war the children and Genek and I lived in our little flat at 32 Rue des Ménapiens in Brussels. It was way too small for a family of four. We only had one bedroom, for one thing. The children slept in cots in our room.

In the back we had a balcony that ran the length of the apartment. To my chagrin Genek insisted on keeping chickens there. He wanted the children to eat fresh eggs. I was horrified. Chickens on my balcony! My husband had no class, honestly. He was a country bumpkin. This was Brussels, not a Polish shtetl. But I couldn't stop him, despite my complaining. He got a chicken coop and a couple of hens, and every day I had to see the mess and the feathers.

What's next, Genek, I said to him, a horse? A cow? But he didn't care what I said. He did what he wanted.

The tiny apartment had running water – a small miracle – but there was no hot water, no private toilet, and no bath. We had to heat water on the stovetop to wash. Once a week Genek took Bobby and they went to the public baths to have a full immersion. I washed Irene in a tin washtub. The toilet was located downstairs from us. We shared this ancient water closet with the family that lived below. We were used to it by now, but sometimes I thought about the splendor in which I had grown up in Chemnitz and I was appalled.

Genek's atelier was upstairs from our living quarters, and he worked there making simple fur garments which we then sold to make a living. Every Shabbos Genek made a big to-do out of going into downtown Brussels to buy his fur scraps. He insisted that Bobby accompany him. He wanted to show off his son. I would watch from the window facing the street as he trundled off with his cart, Bobby seated on the back. This was one of those old-world carts, you know? With the long handles, like you would attach an ox to. But there was no ox. Just Genek, schlepping my child in the cart and walking all the way into downtown Brussels to meet the other old Jewish men and do business.

When they got back, the cart would be full of fur pieces Genek had bought in town. Oh, he loved that weekly errand. It didn't bother him to look like a peasant from the old country. What am I saying? – he was a peasant from the old country. He looked forward to meeting up with the other kakers, all of them survivors, comparing stories, speaking Yiddish in the accents of their native countries. Poles, Germans, Czechs, Hungarians – all of them gathered in a little square downtown, with their wares laid out on tables in the street, bargaining and arguing. Nothing made them happier. And poor Bobby had to go along, so that Genek could tell everyone he was his son, his tachschit, his jewel. I'm sure the child was bored to tears. But Genek was ecstatic.

I helped Genek in the atelier, and Inge did too, until she left for Palestine. Genek cut the furs and made the patterns, and Inge and I sewed. Inge was a skilled seamstress, and she liked the work. And Genek liked having her around, I could tell. My sister was a gentle soul, not a sharp-tongued shrew like me. I think my husband was sweet on her. He always lit up when she arrived, and constantly looked for excuses to come over and chat with her. I chuckled to myself. I wished I was free, or married to a sophisticated man, like the one I had dreamed of as a teenager. I wished sometimes that Genek had married Inge. No doubt he wished that too. But there we were.

I was still very young. In 1945 I was only twenty-four years old. I wanted to live a bit after the years of deprivation during the war. So most nights after we put the kids to bed Genek and I went out – to movies, to cafes, to meet friends, to listen to music, sometimes just to walk the streets of the city. We had been cooped up and in hiding for so long. It was just wonderful to go out freely, without worrying about discovery, arrest, and deportation. We were giddy with freedom.

So we left the children in bed and we went out. It seemed natural. But now that I reflect back I realize how very young they were to be left alone. Bobby was only five, and Irene was just two, when we got them back. And each of them had been traumatized during the war. I didn't think about it then. I assumed they were fine. Of course, later I found out that the children were frightened.

Irene was always a fretful child. It was a relief to me when I could finally put her to bed at the end of the day. I didn't even bother to kiss her goodnight, I am ashamed to say. Bobby, yes, Bobby I adored. I remember one time Bobby asked me, Mama, why don't you kiss Irene goodnight too? But I just couldn't summon the love for the girl. She still rejected me, and I couldn't get over it.

Irene woke up frequently and for comfort she climbed into Bobby's bed. And I know my little boy had bad dreams. I heard him crying in his sleep. I realize now how traumatized he must have been after being separated from us for over two years. Waking up scared and alone while we were out must have been terrible for the children. If they had to use the toilet they had to leave the apartment and climb down a dark cold stairway to the W.C. I know they were so scared at night that they always went to the bathroom together if they had to go. We should have been there to soothe the children when they awoke frightened. But we were selfish.

And of course when we came home there was no privacy. The children slept only a few feet from our bed. I pray they slept soundly.

We tried to live normally. I enrolled Bobby in school. He didn't speak French, but he learned. His first-grade teacher had a soft spot for him. She kept him with her during recess and helped him learn the language. He did fine. Eventually he started playing football and that was an easy way for him to relate to other boys. Bobby always loved sports. I guess he got that from Genek. And you didn't need to be fluent in a language to communicate on the athletic field. Irene was too young to go to school so she stayed home, and either I or Inge or my mother looked after her. Both my sister and mother adored my children. Sometimes Irene played in the atelier while we worked.

Bobby was so fond of my mother that he sometimes took the streetcar across the city to go visit her. By himself. He loved spending time over there, and was spoiled and adored by his grandmother, as well as by Nathan and Inge.

All around us Jewish survivors were talking about emigrating to Palestine. It was a topic of endless conversation. Despite the British blockade, scores of ships were leaving European harbors and steaming toward Palestine. Once Inge had met Hans she immediately started making plans. Surprisingly, my mild-mannered sister became the first in our family to make the journey. My mother and her new husband were talking of emigrating too. And of course Nathan was very eager to go.

It was a real blow when we heard that Nathan's ship had been detained and that he was being interned in Cyprus. We were terribly worried about him. But there was no way to communicate.

Genek, of course, was still trying to find out what had happened to his family back in Lvov. He never did find out exactly how his parents and two brothers died. Nor for that matter what happened to his many cousins and aunts and uncles and friends. We heard about what had happened in Poland, in Galicia. We assumed everyone there was dead. The last communication we had had with them was that telegram when Bobby was born, in April 1940. Genek had cabled his mother the good news, and we had received a reply saying, "congratulations cordiales de bonheur," signed Berta Bottner. So that meant they were alive at that time. But after that, nothing.

It turned out that the entire family had been forced into the Lvov ghetto, where they were issued work cards. Presumably they were eventually sent to one of the death camps from there – likely Belzec. But there were no transport records; no files were ever found. Genek never knew when or where they had perished.

But one day he did find his brother Moshe's name on a Red Cross list. Mundek, his youngest brother, had survived. Genek found out that Mundek was in a D.P. camp. He immediately set off to find him.

A week or so later Genek returned, and with him was Mundek, as well as his Romanian wife Yetta (Tutsa) and their baby daughter Golda. Mundek had survived the war by fighting in the Russian army. And now he had a family. And so three additional people moved into my postage-stamp-sized apartment. All three of them stayed in the living room. And they lived with us for several months until they were finally able to find an apartment of their own.

Living in these overcrowded conditions was intolerable to me. I resented the newcomers terribly. Yetta with her odd eyes, and the baby crying all the time, and just no privacy and no room to breathe. The apartment had been small when it was just me and Genek living in it. But now we had a total of seven people – four adults and three children. And it was too much. I am not proud that I felt this way. I wish I had been different. But this is a true story I'm telling, not a fairy tale. I was happy when they moved out.

And this is very sad too. Genek and Mundek, the only two survivors of their entire family, didn't really get along. I'm sure I contributed to the problem. I was cold and unwelcoming to the young couple. The very last thing in the world I wanted was another Galiciana man living with me; one was more than enough, believe me. And I didn't have anything in common with Tutsa. Bobby adored baby Golda. He played with her and kept her occupied; he was always wonderful with little children. But over the months that we lived together in such proximity, more and more distance developed between our family and Mundek's. A terrible thing. A big regret. Another big regret.

We lived in that apartment in Brussels until late in the winter of 1948. As soon as the first warmth of spring coaxed the daffodils out, we left. That is when we started our journey toward Palestine. The land of Israel was still not established, but we went anyway. We had heard about how austerely the Jews lived in Palestine. So we packed up everything we thought we would want – furniture, a refrigerator, bicycles, dishes, clothes – into a huge wooden crate, and shipped it to Haifa so we would have some creature comforts when we arrived.

My Tante Sarah Gildengoren, my mother's sister, lived in Lyon, France. So Genek, Bobby, Irene, and I left Brussels by train and headed to Lyon. We stayed with Tante Sarah and her family for a week or so. The Gildengorens were also thinking of emigrating to Palestine, and we talked hopefully about the time when we would all reunite, we would be together in what would, God willing, be the land of Israel.

While in Lyon I had the idea that we would want to have a piano in Israel. I was desperate to bring some European culture with me. The piano was a big expense. But I had to have it. So we bought a piano, and made plans to ship it from Lyon to Haifa.

Well, this piano caused a lot of problems. I'm getting ahead of myself here, but let's just say the piano never arrived in Haifa. I don't know what happened exactly, but I do know that Tante Sarah sold the damn piano and kept the money. And that caused a big family rift. It took me years to forgive the Gildengorens for robbing us.

But back to our journey. We made our way to the port of Marseilles, and onto the ship that was to carry us away from Europe. The ship, the Negba, was built to hold 700 people but over 1,800 passengers, all Jewish refugees, crowded the vessel. Many people slept on the decks. The food was terrible. One day I found a worm crawling in my dinner, and I barely ate another morsel for the rest of the seven-day crossing. Luckily the weather was fine. We had smooth sailing and blue skies as we crossed the Mediterranean.

I bunked with three other women. Genek was in a bunk with men. I kept Bobby with me, and Genek took Irene with him. It seems strange to tell the story now. You would think I'd have kept my girl and Genek would have bunked with his boy. But I didn't want to sleep with Irene, nor she with me. She was seasick and I couldn't stand the smell. No, it was better for her to be with her father. Bobby, almost eight years old, slept with me. Anyway, there was no privacy aboard the ship. The women I bunked with were annoyed that I had a boy with me. They yelled at Bobby to turn around every time they wanted to change their clothes. As if he cared about their middle-aged bodies! Poor Bobby – no wonder he spent most of his time on deck.

But we met some nice people on the ship. One particularly was a pleasant young man, maybe nineteen years old. He was traveling by himself. Genek and I befriended him. As we talked, he confided in us that he had a very bad feeling. He knew that when he arrived in Palestine he would be drafted into the Haganah. He was a young male, and the Jewish army was at war with the local Arabs. All young Jewish men were expected to serve in the military, and right away. But this nice boy, he had a bad feeling that something would happen to him. I don't think I'll come out of this, he told us, I have this feeling that I'm going to be killed over there. It was unnerving. We tried to reassure him, but he just shook his head. And don't you know, he was right. A few weeks after we arrived we heard that the poor boy had in fact been killed. I have his face in my mind's eye, but it's terrible, I can't recall his name. Very sad.

At one point, maybe a day or so outside of Haifa, the Negba came to a halt. We noticed the quiet when the ship's engines shut down and, sure enough, we were soon drifting in the sea. Everybody was speculating, worrying about what was going on. Were the British going to board the ship? Would we be sent to Cyprus? To our relief, after a few hours and with no further explanation, the Negba resumed her journey.

I remember, as we approached Haifa we could see sunken ships littering the waters. Masts and broken hulls protruded from the sea, testaments to the fighting that had gone on in the preceding months and years. But we were very lucky. For some reason the British let our ship into Haifa. As we came into harbor I strained my eyes, searching for my sister. Inge was supposed to meet the ship. To my great consternation I couldn't find her.

And of course as we got off the ship there was bedlam. Ecstatic people kissing the ground of the Holy Land, people singing and dancing, and everyone milling around looking for friends and relatives. It turned out Inge was now in the Haganah, and because she was military personnel she couldn't come out to the harbor while the British were patrolling. Eventually Bobby found her. She was among a group of Jewish soldiers in a long bus convoy just adjacent to where we disembarked. Inge and I fell into each other's arms and cried and cried. We had survived, we were reunited, and we were in the land of Israel. It was a very emotional reunion. I don't know how long we clung to each other.

So we arrived in Palestine, and my sister was there, so that was wonderful. But we were not yet free. We were loaded onto buses and the British soldiers escorted us to a nearby detention center, a tent village outside Haifa. We were processed, registered, and issued armbands stating that we were refugees. We lived in those tents for, I don't know, maybe ten days or so. Thank God it was not much longer than that. The place was primitive – no showers, communal toilets – and the heat was oppressive.

Eventually my cousin Miriam, Tante Paula's daughter, who was a native of Palestine, came and vouched for us, and we were released. Miriam brought us back to her house in Nachlat Yehudah, a village just south of Tel Aviv. Miriam had a lovely home. In the backyard was a shed, and Genek and I and the children moved into that shed. We could hear a lot of gunfire and bombing. The children were scared. Once again Irene climbed into bed with Bobby when she needed comfort. We stayed there for about three months.

On May 14, 1948, the country of Israel was born. But despite that wonderful news, the war between the Arabs and Jews went on. The fighting was not over. We still heard artillery and gunshots. Irene still quaked and trembled every time she heard a shot.

Eventually we found our own place to live. It was a farm house in nearby Rishon Le Zion. The owner, Assah, lived upstairs, and we rented out the bottom half of the house. It was very small, but at least the children had their own bedroom. The kids loved it. It was basically like living on a farm, with animals and vegetable gardens and such. It was not at all my cup of tea. The worst part was the thousands of chickens living maybe thirty feet away. They smelt pretty bad in the heat of summer. But even worse, in the winter, when it rained, the mud mixed with the smell of chicken shit was revolting. Really unbearable.

There was a saying in Israel in those times, a word – tzenah. Tzenah means austerity. People had to get used to living austere lives. There were no luxuries. The place was primitive. It was oddly easy for me to minimize the horrors I had lived through in Europe, and to instead remember the cultured luxury that existed there. As I looked around the muddy unpaved roads, the animals living beside me, the squat cement buildings, the crude food, I asked myself, had I made a terrible mistake in coming here?

The crate we had shipped from Brussels miraculously arrived with all our luxuries. So we had an electric refrigerator; we were the only ones around to have that. And Bobby had a bicycle with big balloon tires that was his pride and joy.

But now we had to make ends meet. Genek was a furrier. There was absolutely no chance of him working in the fur business in Israel. So I decided to open a business, a small cafe which I opened together with my mother on Rishon's main street, Rothschild Street. But that business didn't last long. It was a poorly conceived idea. We weren't in Brussels or Antwerp anymore. In newly established Israel people had not the time, the money, or the inclination to buy nice cakes and sip coffee. So we folded up shop and came up with another plan.

Genek and I opened a vegetable stand. Really, it was ridiculous. What did we know about vegetables? Nothing. But we couldn't think of anything better. The infrastructure of the country was a mess, and Genek was the worst businessman. Every day was chaos. The deliveries we ordered didn't always arrive. So sometimes we had vegetables to sell, and other times we didn't. And there was rationing at that time. So we had to redeem people's ration cards when they shopped with us, allotting them three kilos of potatoes, one kilo of tomatoes, whatever it was. But Genek, he was a

Galiciana. He didn't care about the rationing system. If he liked someone he gave them a lot more than he was supposed to. And if he didn't like someone he gave them a lot less. It caused a lot of problems.

Sometimes he lost his temper. Once a woman nagged him, and he took her by the collar and physically threw her out of the store. It was really bad. She complained to the police, and then they came and interviewed Genek about the incident. I couldn't believe it. I thought he was going to be arrested and put in jail. The man was a wild animal, a wilde chaye, I'm telling you.

Food was scarce. We had vegetables from our store, of course, and the chickens from the farm, and eggs. Luckily, my first cousin, Jackie, a tall and strapping soldier, came to visit us often for Shabbos. Jackie would arrive in his army truck carrying a big burlap sack. From the sack he inevitably produced great hunks of meat for me to cook. He pilfered the meat from the army. So that is how we lived.

I felt terribly guilty, but I absolutely hated living in Israel. I wanted to like it, really I did. I supported Israel a hundred percent. Who knew better than me how important it was to have a Jewish homeland? And my family was there – my mother, my sister, my cousins. Eventually even my brother Nathan arrived. But the reality of living there, at that time, with my temperament, was just a terrible fit. And economically we were doing terribly, barely able to pay rent and keep the children fed.

We stuck it out for four years. But I never did learn to love the place. In 1952 we left Israel for Canada. We left behind every family member we had and moved to a country ten thousand miles away where we knew no-one. Everybody was mad at us for leaving, especially Nathan.

But something had broken in me during my life. Maybe it was the constant upheaval, the years of stress and anguish, being married off at age seventeen to a man I didn't love, I don't know. Maybe it was just my nature. But it seemed my destiny was to keep moving for the rest of my life. Friends, community, stability – those were never concepts that I was able to incorporate into my being. I wanted them. I just never achieved them.

END

REFLECTIONS ON A CALAMITY
EPIGENETICS: THE EFFECT OF TRAUMA ON THE DNA

In the introduction I talked about how the relatively new scientific field of epigenetics is producing a new understanding of genetic inheritance. It holds that, while it's true that our genetic makeup is determined entirely by the blueprint that we inherit from our parents, the way that those genes are expressed can be affected by our life experiences. And this leads to changes which we pass on, in turn, to our children.

Think of your genes as a very, very long row of light bulbs. Each bulb represents one gene, and we have millions. Interspersed among these light bulbs are switches. The switches represent points where changes can occur; they can be turned off or on, dimmed or brightened. Those switches are where epigenetics comes in.

Let's pretend we have two identical twins. And let's say one of them smokes two packs of cigarettes per day for thirty years and the other twin doesn't smoke. After thirty years we look at the two and compare them. Remember, identical twins have the same exact genetic makeup. The smoker appears older than his twin, his skin tone is different, and he is ten pounds thinner than the nonsmoker. Why? Because the effects of the cigarettes caused some of his genes to be turned off, others to be turned on, and these changes resulted in different proteins being made in his body. Proteins are little messengers, and so the smoker's body received different genetic messages than that of the nonsmoker twin. What is truly fascinating is that, as a result, the smoker's children will inherit different genetic material than will the nonsmoker's, even though the twins had identical genetic makeup when they were conceived.

So as we go through life, our experiences – stress, happiness, trauma, diet, medications, illnesses, sun exposure, radiation, toxins, exercise patterns – almost everything – affect our genetic expression. On a cellular level this happens because methyl groups bind to certain areas of the gene (the switches), turning it off or on. And the genes can be further affected by histones, the spools around which the DNA is wound. Histones may wind the DNA either tighter or looser, which changes the way the gene is expressed. We can think of histones as the dimmer switches, which can change how brightly a particular light bulb is glowing.

In other words, our environment changes the way our genes are expressed. The old nature versus nurture, or genetics versus environment, question is too simplistic. What we do, how we live, what happens to us, changes how our genes affect us.

And it gets even more interesting now that we know that the differently expressed genes can be passed on to the next generation. The fact that certain lightbulbs have been dimmed or turned on or turned off, results in those modified genes being passed on to the offspring in their slightly altered state.

This is really mind-blowing. What my grandparents experienced in their lives changed their genes. These altered genes were passed on to their child, my father. He, in turn, went through further trauma, food deprivation, and social isolation, further affecting the on/off switches and dimmers, further altering the expression of his genes. And these methylated or altered genes were then passed on to me. So even though I was born in a time of peace and plenty, nonetheless, some of that baggage is literally imprinted in my DNA. And very likely I have passed it on to my own children.

It's not all bad news. The good news is that positive experiences, a healthy diet, exercise, even being in love, can also change our genes – for the better. So even if one inherits a lot of "bad" baggage, what one does in one's own life can modify the effects to some extent. And these positively affected genes are also transmitted to the next generation.

Most people are exposed to a mixture of some good and some bad experiences in their lives. But some people – like the Jews who lived in Europe during World War Two – experienced unprecedented and extreme levels of stress and anxiety. Five years of fear, of hunger, of sensory deprivation, of losing loved ones, of homelessness – five years where each day's survival was an endeavor, five years when stress hormones were sky-high, as they had to be in order to survive – exacted a serious toll on the people, like my family members, who experienced this trauma. And the cumulative effect of this prolonged trauma no doubt created some very significant genetic modifications.

Psychologists and sociologists have studied children of survivors, and found that they exhibit certain behaviors, have more anxiety, than their controls. This finding could be the result of living with traumatized parents (environment). But further studies show that most children of survivors actually have altered cortisone levels (stress hormones), regardless of how they were parented. We can now understand these findings not just as a result of these children having grown up with a parent who had experienced trauma, and having "learned" certain behaviors that resulted from this trauma, but at a genetic level.

There is still much that science has to figure out. Why do some survivors and their children do well, while others suffer from PTSD or other psychological or physical ill effects? There is no easy answer at this point. Studies show that whether one's mother or father underwent trauma, as well as what age they were, affects the progeny's outcomes. And if one looks at grandparents' experiences, it matters whether it is a paternal or maternal grandparent. Strangely, for example, if one's maternal grandmother was severely underfed as a child, one is more likely to develop diabetes but, conversely, if one's paternal grandfather was underfed, the opposite is true. And if one's father was underfed as a child, one is relatively protected from heart disease, but if one's mother was underfed, one is more likely to develop heart disease. The science behind epigenetics and its effect on resilience and health is still in its infancy. But the mere fact that we now understand that life experiences can have an effect on future generations' health is a major step forward in our understanding of how genetics and environment interact in determining our health outcomes.

So, science seems to support quite strongly the hypothesis that I, a child and grandchild of Holocaust survivors, inherited altered genes that affect my cortisone levels, and predispose me to anxiety. Could this predisposition have affected me when my son was born? The time after giving birth is certainly a vulnerable one for most women, so it makes sense that I was affected then. What we don't know is whether there is some kind of collective unconscious memory that is embedded in my DNA, leading me to "remember" the trauma my grandmother Melly was experiencing when her son, my father, was born.

The Nazis invaded Belgium in May of 1940. Soon afterward they began issuing a systematic series of decrees to rob the Jews of their rights. As they did in every country they invaded, their goal was to make the country Judenrein, absent of Jews. This goal was a central tenet of their political strategy. At the time of the invasion, about ninety thousand Jews were living in Belgium, most of them (up to ninety percent) refugees from other countries (Poland, Germany) who had fled ahead of the Nazi occupation.

The big questions, of course, and the ones that are so devastating, are why and how. Why did the Jews become Hitler's scapegoat? How did he succeed in recruiting so much help in his effort to annihilate the Jewish people? Why did so much sadism exist, and why was it turned against a minority that tended to keep to itself and rarely bothered anybody?

There is no ready answer to these philosophical questions, of course. Perhaps, because they were perceived as keeping to themselves rather than integrating into the local population, Jews were an obvious target. Thinking of a group as "other," as lesser, as nonhuman, is a prerequisite for crimes against humanity. Xenophobia is a prerequisite for genocide of a group perceived as racially "other." So a group that lives outside the general community in any way is of course at high risk. Hitler decided that "Jewish blood" was antithetical to his vision of Aryan supremacy – and it didn't matter whether a person practiced Judaism or not. His rabid hatred zeroed in on Jews with laser intensity, and he was able – through persuasion and intimidation – to convince millions of followers to go along.

Jewish people, with their history of valuing education and intelligence more than physical strength, tended to do well economically, at least in Western Europe. Since the Middle Ages, when one of the only professions open to them was banking (money lending), Jews had been associated with money. After World War One, as Germany suffered through a terrible economic depression, the ground was ripe for Hitler to rise, claiming that the Jews were the source of all the Germans' financial troubles, and that getting rid of them would make all their problems go away.

This still begs the question of why millions of people believed this twisted tale and cooperated in the atrocities. Psychological studies have shown that "normal" people can turn sadistic when given absolute control over others. In 1971 a landmark study was conducted by Philip Zimbardo at Stanford University. In this disturbing experiment, a group of college students were split into two groups, and randomly assigned to "be" prisoners or prison guards. The guards were dressed in uniforms and given absolute control over the "prisoners." Within hours the guards turned cruel and sadistic toward their charges, harassing them, humiliating them, and making them do pointless menial tasks, with punishment if they "misbehaved." Perhaps more disturbing, the "prisoners" quickly became submissive and docile, exhibiting "learned helplessness," accepting whatever punishment the guards doled out. This submissiveness in turn seemed to fuel the guards' sadism. Both groups, the aggressors and the persecuted, quickly adopted the "new normal" behaviors of their peers. The experiment was meant to run for two weeks, but after only six days the psychologists had to terminate the study because one researcher realized it was creating a cruel and abusive situation. Zimbardo later noted that he himself did not think to object to what was going on in the "prison." He later stated that he found himself thinking as a prison warden rather than as a psychologist. He too had bought into the new normal reality.

The ramifications of this experiment are deeply troubling. It is terribly disturbing to realize that we humans harbor a dual nature.

Capable of extraordinary kindness and good, we also, unfortunately, are capable of extraordinary sadism and evil when we find ourselves in an environment that supports those traits. And it does not take long for us to adapt to considering another group of people, who days earlier had been our friends and peers, to be inferior and deserving of derision and abuse.

Hitler and his evil empire brought out the very worst side of human nature, with tragic results. In Belgium, even though the Nazis proceeded relatively slowly in their persecution of the Jews, by the fall of 1942, half the Jewish population of Belgium had been rounded up and deported. Another 8,000 Jews, including those of Belgian descent, were rounded up and deported in 1943, rescinding on the promise Hitler had made to Queen Elizabeth that her own Jewish citizens would be safe.

Their belongings were confiscated by the Nazis and transported back to Germany as liebesgaben, spoils of war. Not only were Jewish businesses and homes seized, and used by the Germans and their collaborators, but every valuable object – jewelry, art works, furniture, and home goods – was taken too. This fiscal rape was all part of the Nazi final solution.

Genocide is not new. It had happened time and again prior to World War Two. Nor, sadly, did it end with the Nazi effort to exterminate the Jews. The twentieth century would unfortunately see genocide again, in Cambodia, in Rwanda, and in the Balkans. But the obsessive, maniacal effort that the Nazi party put into annihilating the Jews was unprecedented and has not been equaled since. The construction of an entire infrastructure devoted to documenting, finding, concentrating, transporting, and then gassing and burning six million people, more than a quarter of them children, is impossible to fathom.

For example, the Holocaust claimed the lives of 99.5 percent of the Jews living in Ukraine alone. The chances of surviving the war in this part of the world were abysmal. Over a million Jewish men, women, and children – some estimate more like one and a half million, comparable to the entire population of a city such as San Diego, Phoenix, or Philadelphia – were systematically and brutally beaten, tortured, starved, humiliated, and finally killed. And that number is just in Ukraine. An entire culture was wiped out – a whole world of quirky dark humor, as well as the Yiddish language, destroyed in five years.

Large numbers can be difficult to grasp. How do you comprehend the death of over a million souls? The 9/11 terrorist attacks killed about three thousand people in the U.S.A. If a horror like that happened every day for a year, that would approximate the number of Jews killed in Ukraine during the Holocaust. And if you imagine a 9/11 disaster happening every day for the entire five years of World War Two, with three thousand people dying every one of those days, you would still be half a million short of the six million Jewish deaths at the hands of the Nazis. And – additionally, of course, many other people lost their lives during this terrible time.

The plundering of the Jews' possessions did not end with their death. Guards (or even worse, Jews recruited for the job) scavenged the bodies, pulling gold teeth from the victims' mouths, and sifted through cremated remains looking for jewels the dead may have swallowed before they were killed. Everything of value was confiscated for the Nazis' use.

The Nazis robbed not just the Jews of their humanity; they robbed everyone else of their fundamental decency, in fact of their humanity, as well. Everyone, Jews and non-Jews, was thrust into the impossible choice of either cooperating, or at least passively accepting, the barbarism of the Nazis, or risking their own and their family's annihilation. This was the reality under this savage regime. The Germans made it clear that not only would resisters be brutally punished, but their families would be too. From a comfortably removed perch seventy years later, it is easy to judge.

In such circumstances, it is amazing that still there was a small minority of incredibly brave Resistance fighters who risked everything to fight the fascists, and in doing so salvage their own essential humanity.

The Belgian Resistance movement was comprised of many branches. One, the Independence Front, established the Comité de Défense des Juifs, the CDJ. The CDJ became the main source of protection for the Jews of Belgium, and was responsible, among other tasks, for finding hiding places and organizing the safekeeping of thousands of children. Of the eight founding members of the CDJ, seven were Jewish and one was not; but within a short time many more non-Jews joined the effort. The Independence Front considered the rescue of Jews to be an integral part of their work, and carried this work out under the auspices of the CDJ.

Another of the CDJ's enterprises was forging ration cards and identity papers. The forgeries were so successful, in fact, that the CDJ ended up with more than they needed. They were able to sell the surplus to other resistance movements, as well as to individuals, and to use the money to finance their underground work.

As the roundups began in 1942, parents were faced with this decision: keep their children with them, or give them up and send them into hiding. Many, of course, chose the latter, including Genek and Melly. In sending their children off, hopefully into safekeeping, parents were trusting that their children would escape deportation should a roundup come to their door. At the same time, they realized that they themselves could more easily disappear underground if their children were not with them. Adults could more easily hide than could families with young children. The horror of such a choice is beyond imagination, and speaks volumes about the dire circumstances of the times.

Only the "lucky" ones even got to consider such a choice. Many families were rounded up during the earliest raids in 1942, sent to the detention camp in Malines, and from there deported to the killing camps. They never had a chance to hide, to go underground, or to try to save themselves or their children. My father's Uncle Herman, Aunt Sally, and cousin Joachim, were among that group.

The Jews of Eastern Europe were in even more dire straits. Countries such as Czechoslovakia and Poland were the first to be annexed by the Nazis and the last to be liberated. The Germans were in control there from 1939 to 1945. Compared to countries such as Belgium, the Nazis had two to three additional years of rule in which to implement their sadistic agenda. It was in these countries – as well as in Germany and Austria, of course – that Hitler experimented with ways to shame, intimidate, torture, and kill.

In addition, as mentioned, the local populace in many of those countries was extremely antisemitic and tended to readily join in the torment of their Jewish neighbors. It is not an accident that the Nazis set up the killing camps in Poland. The virulent antisemitism there, and the willingness of (most) of the locals to cooperate in annihilating the Jews, made for a fertile place in which to sow the seeds of evil.

After the war, the very few Jews who had managed to survive were of course homeless and penniless as well as psychologically and physically traumatized. Often having nowhere else to go, some tried to return to their home villages or cities. Many times they knew their families had entrusted valuables to non-Jewish friends and neighbors before entering a ghetto or being deported. Some Jews had buried jewelry and family heirlooms in the ground near their homes, attempting to keep it safe for "after the war." Survivors straggled back, hoping to find some remnant of their family's belongings and to recapture a bit of their fractured lives.

These sorry Jewish refugees, having lost all family and friends, and after being subjected to unspeakable horror and brutality in the camps, were – for the most part – met with further hate if they returned home. After years in exile, the return was a cruel and lonely homecoming, devoid of familiar faces, empty of familiar landmarks. There are heartbreaking accounts of Ukrainian and Polish nationals hissing at returning Jews, spitting at them, expressing shock and dismay that they were still alive. Most Jews found their families' homes and belongings gone – confiscated by their neighbors – never to be returned. Sometimes confrontations broke out, and turned violent. More than one Jew, having somehow survived five years of imprisonment, torture, and unspeakable horror, was killed by villagers upon returning to the place they had once called home.

In addition to physical harassment – the registering, policing, and rounding up of the Jews – the Nazis used other, psychological weapons, and these were perhaps even more sinister. By robbing people of their basic rights – taking away their livelihood, their community, their religion, their homes, and their families, and later their clothes, even their hair – they stripped the Jewish people of their sense of their own essential humanity, rendering them helpless, hopeless, and vulnerable. Vulnerable, terrified people will do whatever they can to feel safe and to survive, including cooperating with the enemy. The Germans, treating Jews as subhuman, forcing them to hide like animals in dens, tried to demonstrate to the world that Jews were useless vermin, ripe for extermination. For some, this became a self-fulfilling prophecy. Sadly, but predictably, some Jews started seeing the Nazis as masters, and themselves as helpless slaves, dumb animals, meekly submitting to any atrocity.

People have a strong and primitive survival instinct. Frightened Jews became increasingly desperate to avoid the wrath of the Nazis and, hoping to survive, did whatever they were told – no matter how horrible or degrading. If told to register, they did. If told to wear gold stars on their clothes, they complied. If told to report for work duty, they showed up. If told to be at a train station at a certain time, together with their children, they were there. If told to dig mass graves before they were shot and pushed into them, they did that too. Told to either help out in the crematoria or end up inside them, some Jews cooperated with the enemy, and helped run the killing camps. This didn't save them, however; most eventually suffered the same fate as those who had gone to the gas chambers before them.

Even after witnessing the brutality of the regime, desperate Jews still hoped that by cooperating with the Germans they would be saved. In 1943, the Nazis managed to "flush out" many of the remaining hidden Jews by announcing that Belgian Jews should now return to their homes, that they were exempt from further actions. Wanting to believe that the worst was over, many came out of hiding. They were, of course, picked up in the next roundups and deported.

It was the rare person who decided not to comply with these orders. It turned out that it was precisely that rare person whose instincts told him not to register, not to wear the star, not to report for work duty, to ignore the many mandates the Nazis imposed – it was that person who would survive. It was those whose instincts told them to hide, to blend in – and who made a thousand lucky choices – who lived to tell the horrific tale of what happened in Europe during the war.

A Child's Experience of the Holocaust

Possibly the most difficult story to tell in this book has been that of my father, Bobby, and his experiences in hiding as a very young child.

A young child experiences time in a very different way to an adult. When you have only been alive for two years, another two years is literally a lifetime.

Young children are meant to be loved, to be nurtured, and to have a lot of sensory input – sights, sounds, smells, tastes, and touch. They learn by exploring their environment, by exploring their senses. Their brain development depends on this input. The world in which Bobby found himself was deficient in all of these areas. The world of the Jewish children hidden in a convent was one of sensory deprivation.

Their room was in the basement, poorly lit, sometimes completely dark. There were no toys, no bright objects, no sunlight, no green plants, no crayons, no paint, no picture books. There were no windows to look out of. Bobby recalls the world existing in shades of gray. He experienced a world deprived of color and visual stimulation. He literally forgot that color existed. His first memory of noticing color is after the war. His years in the convent were gray ones.

The nuns insisted the boys keep quiet. If the Germans came around, as they sometimes did, they must not hear the sound of childish voices, they must not be alerted to a room of hidden children. So Bobby and the other hidden children lived in a world of silence, deprived of music, of song, of normal human voices other than the occasional whisper. Perhaps the nuns responded to the children's cries, perhaps they didn't. Children raised in orphanages where their cries are ignored eventually stop crying. Decades later, in Romania, psychologists noted that in orphanages in that country there existed an eerie silence: rows of babies lying soundlessly in their cribs. There was no point in making sound if nobody listened, nobody responded. Bobby's years in the convent were silent ones.

Food was scarce. The children were fed enough to be kept alive, but there was no exploration of the sense of taste. Maybe they received some lumpy porridge, some stale bread, some tasteless soup. But their diet was deficient, both nutritionally and sensorially. Of course, there were no sweets or treats. Food did not exist as a sensory delight; the children were lucky to have some caloric intake, and that was all. Bobby's years in the convent were hungry ones.

Taste is intimately connected to smell, and in the underground world of the convent there was a paucity of scents. No flowers to smell, no aroma of baking cookies or roasting chicken, not even the scent of a spring rain or the comforting aroma of a mother's skin for these children. The only smell was one of damp, of mold growing on the walls of the convent.

And finally, not enough touch. Children thrive when they are held, hugged; they need human touch to develop. The hidden children of the convent received only perfunctory touch from the nuns who cared for them, but they missed out on the intimacy of being lovingly held. Instead, they lived in a cold damp environment, with insufficient clothing to withstand the winter chill. They had no cozy blankets or stuffed toys to cuddle, no sand to sift through their fingers, no grass to explore with their toes, no warm body to nestle into. The lack of loving human touch was perhaps the worst of the sensory deprivations for the youngsters.

Young children need not just sensory input, but love and attention in order to grow and develop normally. Institutionalized children do not grow properly: their height, weight, and head circumference measurements are usually too low, a condition called "failure to thrive." Even with adequate nutrition (which the hidden children did not have) the lack of intimacy prevents children from growing. They are literally stunted by despair. Additionally, institutionalized children often exhibit delayed speech, poor fine and gross motor skills, intellectual impairment, abnormal socialization, atypical behaviors, and a host of psychological problems. They do not develop normally, either physically or emotionally.

Children who grow up in large orphanages may not have access to what they need at critical times in their development. Babies require a unique bond with their mother (or another adult) in order to develop empathy and normal social behavior. This is called attachment. Babies with abnormal attachment in infancy have a lot of difficulty forming normal relationships later in life.

Luckily for Bobby, his first two years of life had been spent in a loving family environment, allowing his most critical development to occur normally. But for the next two and a half years he was cut off from loved ones and insufficiently fed, and he existed in a cold and lonely world of sensory deprivation. He did survive, but the stress of the ordeal no doubt left its mark on his psyche, his health, and – as the discussion of epigenetics shows – also on his genes. These genes would be the ones he would someday pass on to his own children. We cannot know for sure exactly how the genes that he passed on might have been altered by his experiences. But unquestionably, such trauma, such sensory and emotional deprivation, so early in his life, profoundly influenced who Bobby was as a person, and it is certainly possibly that this influence was profound enough to affect his genetic inheritance.

The Complicated Politics of Palestine/Israel

After the horrors of the Holocaust, there was one crucial event that rose from the ashes of World War Two: the formation of a Jewish homeland in Israel. After two thousand years without refuge from oppression, the Jewish people finally had a place of unconditional sanctuary.

The land of Israel is tiny and it is vulnerable, but the fact that it exists at all is no small miracle. To understand the complicated politics of the region and how Israel came to be, it is necessary to review a little history.

At the end of World War One, the British, victorious over the Ottoman Empire – which had fought on the German side – ousted the Turks and assumed control over much of the Middle East, including the area called Palestine. This small strip of land had been coveted and fought over for millennia. Sacred to Christians, Muslims, and Jews, and right in the middle of the trade routes between Africa and Asia, wars and turmoil had repeatedly wracked this tiny geographical space.

When the British inherited control of this area in 1919 there were already stirrings between the local Jewish and Arab populations, each of which lay claim to the territory as their ancestral homeland, and both of which wanted independent rule.

The Jewish Zionist movement was burgeoning in Europe, founded by Theodor Hertzl, a journalist from Vienna. He and his followers, responding to centuries of antisemitic persecution, were determined to create a Jewish homeland. As the movement took hold, thousands of Jews in the Diaspora seized upon the idea of a Jewish state in the ancient land of Israel, where Jews could live in safety and dignity. In the late nineteenth century European Jews began emigrating to Palestine, purchasing land and establishing Jewish settlements and kibbutzim. The Palestinian Arab community, threatened by this Jewish influx, established the Arab National Congress, which supported the rights of Arabs to self-rule.

Britain, caught uncomfortably between the two groups, tried to placate them by promising both sides what they wanted. In 1914, the British promised the Arabs independent rule in exchange for military support against the Ottomans. But after the war the British issued the Balfour Declaration, promising the Jewish people an independent Jewish state. Clearly these two promises were contradictory. In the ensuing decades relations deteriorated between Jews, Arabs, and the British who ruled them.

In 1929 the Jewish Agency was established, led by Chaim Weitzman. This agency was created in response to a decision made by the League of Nations (the predecessor to the United Nations), calling for representatives of Jews from around the world to assist in the creation of a Jewish state.

In 1936 the Arabs staged a revolt in Palestine, which lasted for three years. The Arab Revolt was aimed at the British rulers and the Jewish locals, through general strikes as well as violent incursions. The aim was to oust the British and regain autonomy. In response, Neville Chamberlain, the British prime minister, issued the White Paper of 1939, which attempted to placate the Arabs. The White Paper stated that Palestinian support would be required for the formation of any Jewish state in the region. And, crucially, it limited Jewish immigration to 15,000 annually for the next five years, and placed restrictions on Jews' rights to buy land from the Arabs. The immigration restriction's timing was particularly troubling as Hitler was ascending to power and Jews in Europe were facing ever more dangerous times.

But then World War Two began and British attentions were drawn elsewhere. The Arab Palestinians, led by Grand Mufti Husseini, sided with the Germans and Italians during the war. Husseini, in fact, met personally with Hitler, and is said to have been given a tour of Auschwitz. The Jewish population, on the other hand, served in the British army and loyally fought in Europe against the Germans.

Much to their dismay, at the conclusion of the war, the British, exhausted by war but responsible for the areas they had colonized, faced several areas of turmoil within their empire. One of those was in Palestine. The Nazi Holocaust had wiped out six million Jews in Europe. The survivors of the camps and ghettos were displaced refugees, many of whom longed to resettle in the land of Israel and work toward the formation of an independent Jewish state. Many of these people, homeless, were housed in refugee camps all over

Europe, many even in Germany, which was particularly intolerable. International outrage put pressure on the British to allow these Jews entry into the Palestinian mandate. But at the same time, Arab leaders, vehemently resistant to the establishment of a Jewish state, put pressure on Britain to resist this decision.

The White Paper of 1939 had set up quotas for Jewish immigration into the country. Britain was faced with the choice between implementing this law, turning away illegal ships carrying Jewish refugees from Europe, or warring with the local Palestinian Arabs and the other Arab countries in the Middle East. My family was among the refugees caught in this international tug-of-war.

For several years Britain opted to enforce the Jewish immigration quotas. Desperate Jews, however, continued to stream toward the land of Israel, crowding onto barely seaworthy ships in European ports and crossing the Mediterranean. Intercepting these illegal ships, the British then had to decide what to do with all the Jewish refugees.

Their solution was to create internment camps on the island of Cyprus, also under British rule. Cyprus is about 300 miles northwest of Israel, an arid island approximately eighty miles long. Eventually thirty-nine ships carrying a total of over fifty thousand desperate people were intercepted and rerouted to Cyprus after World War Two. There, impromptu tent villages surrounded by barbed wire and guarded by armed soldiers housed the refugees. Eventually more camps were built, some with tents, others with long crude barracks covered by semi-circular tin roofs. Some of the Jewish refugees, many of whom had survived the Nazi killing camps in Europe, were to spend several more years as prisoners of the British army in Cyprus.

At the peak of this period there were nine camps in Cyprus, located at two sites fifty miles apart. One was in Karalos, near Famagusta; the other was at Dekhelia, near Larnaca. Nathan was housed in Camp 68 in the Dekhelia area. While no atrocities were committed in these camps – unlike in those of Europe – the inmates were prisoners nonetheless. They were housed in rude barracks surrounded by barbed-wire fences. Food and water shortages, lack of hygienic facilities, lack of heat or cooling, and above all, lack of dignity, were the norm.

The situation was particularly excruciating for those who had survived Nazi concentration camps, as Shoshana had. One can only imagine the despair they felt at once again being imprisoned, once again living in a camp, once again seeing towers with armed guards preventing their escape. These internment camps were in use from 1946 until 1949, when the last prisoners were finally allowed to leave for the newly established state, Israel. Nathan, as a young fit male of fighting age, was one of the last to be released from the camps. He didn't arrive in Israel until eight months after it was declared an independent state.

When World War Two came to an end, the British, financially and emotionally spent and less inclined toward colonial rule, turned the decision of what to do in Palestine over to the newly formed United Nations. The UN met on November 29, 1947, and, in a historic vote, decided to partition Palestine into a Jewish state (Israel) and an Arab state (Trans-Jordan). This resolution, number 181, called for the city of Jerusalem to be an international zone. Resolution 181 called for the progressive withdrawal of the British from the area.

The resolution was accepted by the Jews but rejected by the Arabs. Even as Jews danced around bonfires and celebrated in the streets, outraged Arabs prepared to fight, and war broke out almost immediately. The Jews called the subsequent war, which lasted well into 1948, the War for Independence. The Arabs called it the Catastrophe. Nevertheless, on May 14, 1948, as the British finally withdrew from the country, David Ben-Gurion, head of the Jewish Agency, proclaimed the creation of the Jewish State of Israel. After two thousand years without a homeland, after six years of Nazi atrocities, and despite universal Arab opposition, the Jews finally had a country of their own.

In the twenty-first century it has become mainstream to criticize Israel. And, certainly, it is a country with a lot of problems. But Israel is a tiny nation-state, only a few miles wide in some spots, and it is the only place in the world that guarantees that another Holocaust will not happen to the Jewish people. Every Jew in the world is welcome to resettle in Israel. The value of this safety net is, hopefully, evident after reading about the events that took place in Europe in the last century.

Moreover, I would argue that it is hypocritical of Europeans and Americans to voice outrage about territorial disputes in a tiny country most know very little about. For one thing, European nations themselves have a pretty checkered history. Many colonized the developing world and shamelessly exploited the natural resources in each country, and did so until fairly recently. When it was time to withdraw from its colonies, Europe handily carved up areas, renamed them, and reassigned inhabitants at will. An example of this is the partition of India by the British in 1948, the creation of Pakistan and Bangladesh, and the resettlement of millions of people. And let's not forget that the country now called the United States was, in fact, inhabited when the European settlers arrived a few centuries ago. The way the Native Americans were treated by the invaders, the way an entire continent of land was stolen from them, the way they were pushed to the brink of extinction, is a travesty that gets relatively little attention. My point is not to minimize the very real problems that exist in Israel, but to question the self-righteous judgment that often rains down on the state.

Israel is not perfect. I would argue that no country is. But it is certainly not the world's great villain. It is a small and complicated place wrestling with the uneasy task of juggling the needs of many diverse people with conflicting agendas. But whatever it does, right or wrong, it is a unique haven for a people who desperately need one, and who have no other place that they can ultimately call their own. And for that alone Israel deserves the support of the world.

EPILOGUE
SURVIVAL

Gertrude

Gertrude spent the rest of her life in Israel. After the death of her second husband Shlomo Kliegsberg, whom her family adored, she married for the third time. Her third husband was ultra-religious and stern, an echo perhaps of her first husband. She lived to see her great-grandchildren thriving and free in the land of Israel. She passed away at the age of seventy-seven.

Nathan and Shoshana

Nathan and Shoshana also remained in Israel, both serving in the new Israeli army, the IDF. Nathan went on to have a career in the IDF. They had two sons, Arik and Ronnie, and at the time of writing are both still alive and well and enjoying their grandchildren, great-grandchildren, and many friends. Nathan continues the swimming habit his father instilled in him; he and Shoshana still swim for exercise every morning. At age eighty-nine Nathan is still sharp and his memory astounding.

Inge and Hans

Inge and Hans lived happily in Israel for the rest of their lives. Both now deceased, they are survived by their son Ami, four grandchildren, and several great-grandchildren. Ami, married to a lovely woman named Judith, is every bit as kind and sweet as his parents were.

Irene

Irene's early childhood trauma caused a permanent rift between her and her parents, particularly between her and Melly. The two never got along. Irene recalls feeling like an outsider as a child, ruefully witnessing the love she saw her parents lavish on her brother Bobby.

"I didn't really have a childhood," she remembers. "It wasn't just the war. It was the constant moving, the different schools, the new countries all the time, the new languages. I never had continuity." She was treated more as hired help than as a daughter. As a teenager she was expected to come straight home after school, clean the house, and cook for the family. She felt isolated, lonely, and very unhappy for the entire first two decades of her life. Her brother was the only one she felt close to.

She never saw her "Namur family" again. It wasn't until many decades later that she was able to find information about who exactly they were. By then her adopted parents had both died. Monsieur Bouchat, she was told, passed away holding a photograph of little Irene in his hand. He never got over the loss of the little girl he loved and whom he never saw again after her parents came to get her when she was two.

When Irene was twenty, Bobby suggested his sister pay a visit to her family back in Israel, to get out of Ottawa and to escape her unhappiness at home for a while. Irene thought this was a splendid

228

idea. She bought a ticket to Israel and spent a year living with Inge and Hans and their young son, Ami. This trip would be pivotal in her life. In fact, what started as a vacation became a permanent relocation.

"That was the happiest year of my life", Irene recalls. "Inge gave me all the love my mother never did. I felt completely welcome and I became one of the family. Ami became my little brother." She actually had to share a bed with the then eleven-year-old Ami as there was nowhere else for her to sleep. But she was ecstatic. She tried to pay Inge and Hans back by lavishing gifts on Ami, and buying treats and delicacies to bring home on Shabbos.

Shortly after arriving in Israel she met a young man named Shlomo Wechsler, a native of the country, a sabra. "Shlomo also gave me affection ... he only gave me good things and love. He made me feel good. And his family too. They loved me. They became my family." The two were married in 1963, remained in Israel, and had two children – a son, Ronnie, and a daughter, Nurit. They now have five grandchildren and are enjoying their retirement in a suburb of Tel Aviv.

Melly and Genek

Melly and Genek remained in their troubled marriage. Their love life was not the only area in which they were unmoored. For the rest of their lives they struggled to find a place to call home. Theirs was a nomadic life. After leaving Israel they lived for several years in Montreal, then moved to Ottawa, and eventually back to Israel. But, unable to find peace, they left again and repeated the entire moving sequence. At one point they even moved to western Canada, living in Calgary for a couple of years.

While living in Canada, Genek was able to pursue his career in the fur business, first in Montreal and then in Ottawa. Melly was his business partner. She made contacts, delivered furs, and kept the books. Eventually Bobby was enlisted to help with the driving errands for the business, as Genek never did learn to drive. Bobby traveled all over Quebec to pick up and deliver goods. He was only thirteen years old when he started driving, many years before he was legally eligible to get his license. In Ottawa, the couple owned a successful fur store called Elite Furs. But they gave up this store to relocate back to Israel in the mid-1960s, following Bobby, who had already moved back. Maybe they never got over the guilt of abandoning their boy, or their desire to make it up to him. Where he went, they followed.

Over the years Melly became overweight and developed diabetes, high blood pressure, and arthritis. She started smoking cigarettes, a habit she was never able to kick. Although not formally diagnosed, she suffered from depression. She never seemed depressed when I was around her, though. She came alive when my parents, my sister, and I came to visit.

When she was sixty-four she suffered a major heart attack. Irene flew back from Israel to see her mother. It was during this final visit that Melly finally apologized for the way she had treated Irene as a child. Bobby begged his mother to find the strength to live, but she was weakening. She held on until her beloved sister Inge arrived from Israel, and then died in Inge's arms. Ironically, Melly's final wish was to be buried in Israel, the country she had been unable to find peace in during her lifetime. Bobby transported her body to Israel and arranged for the burial to happen there.

Although, at sixty-four, she died very young by today's standards, I was already twenty-two when my grandmother passed away. So I knew her well. To me she seemed like an accomplished, sophisticated, loving, and fascinating grandmother. She lavished my sister and I with presents every Rosh Hashanah and Passover. She prepared elaborate meals and knit us beautiful sweaters. She was intelligent, sensitive, and wise, with a wry smile and a kind heart. I don't recall seeing her sad exactly, but pensive and fretful, yes. What was clear was that she adored us. I realize now there were not many things she considered precious in her life, but her granddaughters, my sister and I, were certainly that.

My grandfather Genek adored us too and, moreover, he made us laugh. He even made Melly laugh at times. He was a wise-cracking, fun-loving jokester. His humor was wrapped up in his Yiddish roots, full of colorful one-liners and idioms that defy translation. Everything was a bit of a joke to Genek. He never stopped repeating his favorite lines, some of which have become family sayings in my home. It's better to throw in than to throw out, my husband and I joke when we tuck into leftovers. And whenever I cook with garlic, I give an inner chuckle, thinking about my Saba's chortling repetition – if you eat garlic every day for a hundred years, you will live a long time.

After Melly's death in 1986 Genek was at a loss. He moved back to Israel again, and remained there for the rest of his life. Despite his problematic relationship with Irene, he asked her to quit her job so she could keep house and cook for him. Although she refused, Irene did help take care of him for the rest of his life.

As he got older Genek's mind deteriorated. He found himself perseverating about what had happened during the war. As he slipped into dementia he was tormented by memories of losing his family, recalling little of his recent life, but having all-too-clear memories of what the Nazis had done when he was young. He died in 1997 at the age of eighty-six.

Bobby

My father (called Al by everyone other than his family of origin) went to high school in Montreal, and then attended engineering college in Ottawa. When he was nineteen he met the love his life, young Rosalee Segal, and the two became an item. They were married two years later and produced a daughter, me, a year after that. But Dad was to emulate the restlessness that was his parents' lifestyle.

My parents left Ottawa only a few months after my birth, leaving my mother's family behind, and starting what would become the long search for the right place to call home. They lived briefly in Puerto Rico, then Chicago, before moving to Israel in 1966. My sister Sharon was born there a couple of months after we arrived.

We lived in Israel for six years. I went to school there, became fluent in Hebrew, learning how to read and write it well before I did English. My dad served in the IDF, a bit of an ordeal as he was several years older than the rest – almost all eighteen-year-old boys – and had a family at home. But he went through the six-week basic training and then served in the Reserves as all Israeli men did. I remember him kissing me goodbye before he left for basic training, and I recall crying and crying, heartbroken that my foreign-looking uniform-clad daddy was going off to be a soldier. I was terrified.

In 1967 when the Six Day War broke out, my father was called up. My recollection of that war is of air-raid sirens going off, and of having to immediately rush down to the basement of our apartment building. Everyone who lived in the building, twelve families, sought shelter down there. It was cool and damp and dim, but there was a ping-pong table and people didn't seem overly frightened. The adults brought food and chatted. The kids played. We had to stay in the cement basement until the all-clear siren went off. The only time I was really scared was one day when I was playing with a neighbor, a boy named Zvika, and the siren went off. Zvika's mother grabbed each of us kids by the hand and literally ran down the stairs, so fast that I was unable to keep up. She dragged us down to the shelter as we slipped haphazardly on the stairs. To me, her evident fear was scary.

Little did I know that there was ample reason to be afraid. The armies of three Arab countries, Syria, Jordan, and Egypt, were at war with Israel's tiny IDF. A thousand Israeli soldiers would die in this war. My dad contributed to the war effort primarily via his engineering skills.

But when I was eight years old my father decided we should leave Israel, and we moved to England. This move mirrored the one that Bobby had experienced with his parents when he was a child. Just like them, he uprooted his family from the country he loved and believed in completely, to move thousands of miles away to a place where they knew no-one. His children would not grow up with their cousins, aunts, and uncles nearby. Despite his passion for Israel, Bobby left.

After two years in England we moved to the U.S. We eventually settled in a Boston suburb, where we lived until Sharon and I graduated from high school. Interestingly, my grandparents, Melly and Genek, left Israel again too once we were in Boston, and moved "nearby," settling in Montreal – again. But as soon as Sharon and I were both in college, my parents moved on once again – first to the San Francisco area and later to Florida. Even in Florida they changed homes many times.

When he was in his late fifties my dad retired from engineering and started working as a travel agent in Sarasota, Florida. Fluent in five languages and having lived in Europe, Canada, and Israel, he was quite successful, and enjoyed putting together interesting itineraries for his clients. He sometimes even went along on some trips as a guide.

One day in 1997 when Dad was working at his desk at VIP World Travel, a client came in to ask for help arranging a trip for himself and his wife. The client, a British man, was named Tony Hayes. As he and my dad chatted, they discovered some interesting coincidences. Hayes, then working as an air traffic controller, was based in Brussels where my dad had lived as a child. And, strangely, he and his wife lived on Rue des Ménapiens – the very same street my dad had lived on many decades earlier. The two got to sharing stories, and my dad told Hayes a little of his background and what his family had been through during World War Two. Hayes was fascinated.

Six months later, when he was again in Sarasota, Hayes returned to the travel agency to visit my dad. He brought with him a copy of a magazine called The Bulletin, an English-language publication from Brussels, and tossed it onto my dad's desk. Thought you might be interested in this, Al, he told him, there's a story about Jewish children who were hidden and saved during World War Two in Belgium.

My dad started leafing through the magazine, interested, of course, in the story. Suddenly he stopped. Included in the article was an old photograph. The photo was in black and white, and showed a group of little boys all dressed alike, standing in rows, with two nuns beside them. My dad peered at the photo. Oh my God, he said. This is me. I am in this photo. Hayes was incredulous. But it was true. The photo, which my dad had not known was in existence, showed him as a four-year-old child, while he was in hiding in the convent in Banneux more than fifty years before. It was as if decades of time had suddenly been peeled back, transporting my dad to a time and place he thought he would never visit again.

Several months later my dad traveled to Europe as a tour guide. One of his stops was in Brussels. Dad had contacted Tony Hayes to let him know he would be coming to town, and Hayes had insisted they meet for a beer. My dad was on a tight schedule, but Hayes assured him he would come to the Sheraton Hotel in Brussels where the group was staying, and visit him there. Sure enough, one evening after an arduous day of travel, my dad got a call that Hayes was in the lobby waiting for him. My dad, weary but not wanting to disappoint his new friend, took a quick shower, and went down to the lobby to meet him. But Hayes was not alone. With him he had brought a journalist, Vivien Teitelbaum, the author of the article in The Bulletin where Dad had seen a photo of himself as a hidden child. Another woman, a photographer for the magazine, was with them as well.

They explained to my dad that Hayes had contacted them and told them he had serendipitously found one of the hidden children in the photo. The author wanted to interview Dad and write a follow-up piece. Soon the lobby of the Sheraton was cleared, much to my dad's amazement, as the photographer started snapping photos of him being interviewed by Vivien Teitelbaum. Dad laughs as he recounts the story. They must have thought there was a real celebrity there! On September 24, 1998, a feature article entitled, "How did you survive the war, daddy?" ran in The Bulletin, recounting my dad's survival story, and featuring a contemporary photo of him sitting on a sofa with Teitelbaum, as well as the original photograph of him as a hidden child in the convent.

Several years later, my parents returned to Belgium again. My dad was becoming more and more interested in learning what he could about what had happened in Belgium during World War Two, and he wanted to see the places he had lived as a child. They discovered that the Holocaust Museum was now housed in Mechelen – also known as Malines, the site of the transit camp where Belgian Jews were imprisoned awaiting transport to Auschwitz. My parents took the train to Mechelen, located halfway between Brussels and Antwerp, the cities that had been home to most of the Jewish population in Belgium before the war. Mechelen, my dad noted, is located right on the train tracks.

My parents started walking around the museum. At one point they wandered away from each other, looking at different things. Suddenly, my mother's voice shattered the hushed atmosphere of the somber museum. Al, she called, Al, come here, your picture is on the wall. Sure enough, the very photograph that had been included in the article in The Bulletin was hanging on the wall in

Mechelen. My parents gazed at the blown-up version of the row of little boys. One boy, not my dad, had a blue light shining on his photo. They later learned that that light signified that the child had been identified as an adult survivor.

The discovery of another actual survivor shown in a photo on exhibit caused a bit of a stir at the museum. My parents met the curator, who told my dad he was only the second person to be identified from the photo of the hidden children. She promised she would arrange to have his face illuminated in the future. She also introduced my parents to a researcher who ushered them into her office to talk. This was when my dad learned the identity of the person who had picked him up from his parents' apartment when he was a very young child and transported him into hiding in the convent, Andree Geulen. She was now getting on in years, but still fully cognizant, and living in Brussels. The researcher showed my dad documentation from Andree's notebooks. He gazed in astonishment at the records written in longhand. He had been Child 1068. His sister Irene had been Child 1069. Again, what had seemed like a long-lost watery dream came back in clear bold strokes.

My dad called Andree Geulen, and my parents arranged to visit her in her apartment in Brussels. They found her to be incredibly youthful, welcoming, and engaging on their visit, the day of her eighty-fifth birthday. They spent three hours together. She told my dad that she was in close contact with many of the people she had helped save when they were children. Quite a few of them now resided in Israel; others were scattered around the world. In fact, during my parents' visit, several of them called to chat with the octogenarian and wish her a happy birthday. Andree told my dad about what it was like during the war, how the Resistance worked to hide the Jewish children, and about her memories of transporting the young kids away from their parents. She even had her notebooks, where she had kept track of all the children she helped hide, in her apartment. She showed my parents the very entry showing that Child 1068, Alfred Bottner, code name Bobby, had been picked up, and brought into hiding in 1942 and again in 1943.

Over the years, Andree had been recognized and lauded for her work saving children, even receiving the prestigious recognition from Israel as one of the Righteous Amongst the Nations. But let me show you what I am most proud of, she told my parents, before they left, leading them to a room where a plaque hung on the wall. This award is my pride and joy, she beamed. The award was from the City of Brussels. On it was engraved, "Mensch of the Year."

Now, finally, in their seventies, my parents have stopped moving. They live in Sarasota and seem content in their retirement. Their four grandchildren – my children, Ari and Sophia, and Sharon's children, Alena and Jacob – are their pride and joy. Dad misses his family in Israel, particularly his sister Irene, and his uncle Nathan, who is like an older brother to him. After my trip to Israel in 2016 I convinced my parents to return for an overdue visit, and they happily reunited with the extended clan.

And so the family survived. Through intuition, chutzpah, and a lot of good luck, those who lived through the darkest times of the European Holocaust managed to evade annihilation. Their descendants – including myself – are here due to their courage.

We owe them all a debt of gratitude. But survival had a price. I believe we inherited their pain and suffering too, and it is embedded in our DNA.

DESCENDANTS OF LEOPOLD AND GERTRUDE OFFNER

FULL FAMILY TREE

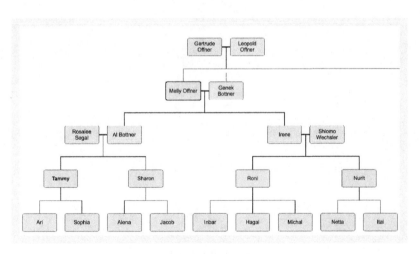

Melly's Descendants

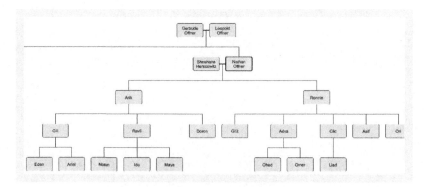

Nathan's Descendants

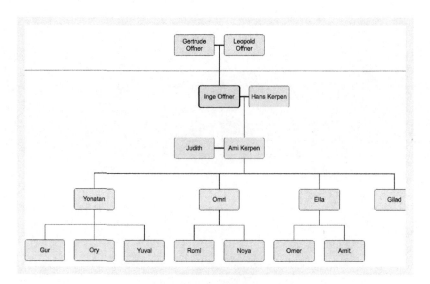

Inge's Descendants

SOURCES AND FURTHER READING

Prologue

Tracing family heritage and Jewish archives: JewishGen website. www.jewishgen.org.

Center for Holocaust and Genocide Studies. 2017. "Collections & Exhibitions." College of Liberal Arts. University of Minnesota. https://cla.umn.edu/chgs/collections-exhibitions.

Genek: Lvov, 1920s and 1930s

Jewish Virtual Library. "Virtual Jewish World: Lvov, Ukraine." www.jewishvirtuallibrary.org/lvov-ukraine-jewish-history-tour.

Sport in Lvov:

Godfrey, Mark. 2016 (May 18). "Jewish Clubs of Inter-War Poland: Makkabi Warszawa." The Football Pink.

Jacobs, Jack. 2010. "Sport: An Overview." YIVO Encyclopedia of Jews in Eastern Europe.

www.yivoencyclopedia.org/article.aspx/Sport/An_Overview.

Lviv Interactive. "Vul. Zolota, 32 – Stadium." www.lvivcenter.org/en/lia/objects/?ci_objectid=1972.

Rightbankwarsaw. 2013 (January 26). "Jewish Football in Inter-War Warsaw: Gwiazda-Sztern Warsaw."

https://rightbankwarsaw.com/2013/01/26/jewish-football-in-inter-war-warsaw-gwiazda-sztern-warszawa/.

Rightbankwarsaw. 2013 (December 1). "Ukraina Lviv. The Story of Ukrainian Football in Inter-war Poland."

https://rightbankwarsaw.com/2013/12/01/ukraina-lviv-the-story-of-ukrainian-football-in-inter-war-poland/.

Stephen Spielberg Film and Video Archive. "Maccabi Atheletes in Antwerp." United States Holocaust Memorial Museum. www.ushmm.org/online/film/display/detail.php?file_num=4570.

Wikipedia. 2016 (October 25). "Pogoń Lwów (1904)." https://en.wikipedia.org/wiki/Pogo%C5%84_Lw%C3%B3w_(1904).

Yad Vashem. 2017. "Jews and Sport before the Holocaust: A Visual Retrospective." www.yadvashem.org/yv/en/exhibitions/sport/index.asp.

The Maccabi Games reinstated:

Axelrod, Toby 2015 (July 21). "European Maccabi Games to Be Held at Olympic Venues Built by Nazis." Jewish Telegraphic Agency. www.jta.org/2015/07/21/news-opinion/world/european-maccabi-games-to-play-at-olympic-venues-built-by-nazis.

Modern-day Lviv:

Apelsyn (Tour Operator). 2013. "The Juice: Lviv." http://apelsyn.com/en/news-view/items/the-juice-lviv.html.

German Occupation: Belgium, 1940–1941

Gershon-Lehrer.be (blog). 2012 (July 5). "Expulsion Orders from WWII at the FelixArchief – Part 2: Researching The Inventory." www.gershon-lehrer.be/blog/tag/holocaust-2/.

Wikipedia. 2017 (January 11). "German Occupation of Belgium during World War II." https://en.wikipedia.org/wiki/German_occupation_of_Belgium_during_World_War_II#Life_in_occupied_Belgium.

Melly: Life under Occupation

The Anti-Jewish Laws: Belgium, 1942

Holocaust Survivors.org. "Survivor Stories: Joseph Sher." www.holocaustsurvivors.org/data.show.php?di=record&da=survivors&ke=2.

Hunt, Kyle (producer and editor). 2015. "Hellstorm – Exposing the Real Genocide of Nazi Germany." www.youtube.com/watch?v=qkQ6J5Fo1Do; www.hellstormdocumentary.com.

United States Holocaust Memorial Museum. "Jews in Prewar Germany."

www.ushmm.org/outreach/en/article.php?ModuleId=10007687.

Andree Geulen and the Resistance: September 1942

Abramowicz, Myriam and Esther Hoffenberg (directors). 1980. "Comme si c'était hier [As If It Were Yesterday]." The National Center for Jewish Film.

Bolinger, Bruce. 2003. "Dutch and Belgian Heroism – Part I." WWII Netherlands Escape Lines. https://wwii-netherlands-escape-lines.com/airmen-helped/articles-about-the-line/dutch-and-belgian-heroism-part-one/.

Dumont, Frédéric (director) and Willy Perelsztejn. 2003. "Just a Link." Les Films de la Mémoire.

Belgium and Holland, 1943

Holocaust Education & Archive Research Team. 2015. "Apeldoornse Bos: Deportation of Psychiatric Patients to Auschwitz-Birkenau." Holocaust Research Project.

www.holocaustresearchproject.org/nazioccupation/apeldoornsebos.html.

Bobby: 1942 and 1943

Isaacman, Clara. 1984. Clara's Story. As told to Joan Adess Grossman. The Jewish Publication Society.

Kisliuk, Ingrid. 1988. Unveiled Shadows: The Witness of a Child. Nanomir Press.

Loebl, Suzanne. 1997. At the Mercy of Strangers: Growing Up on the edge of the Holocaust. Pacifica Press.

Marks, Jane. 1993. The Hidden Children: The Secret Survivors of the Holocaust. Fawcett Columbine.

To Life: Stories of Courage and Survival, Told by Hampton Roads Holocaust Survivors, Liberators and Rescuers. United Jewish Federation of Tidewater, Virginia Beach, VA.

Vromen, Suzanne. 2008. Hidden Children of the Holocaust: Belgian Nuns and Their Daring Rescue of Young Jews from the Nazis. Oxford University Press.

In Hiding: Banneux, 1943

Wikipedia (France). 2015 (June 13). "Albert Van den Berg (résistant)."

https://fr.wikipedia.org/wiki/
Albert_Van_den_Berg_(r%C3%A9sistant).

Back in Lvov

Europe Between East and West (blog). 2015 (November 18). "Traces of the Golden Rose Synagogue – Beyond the End of a History in Lviv (Part One – Text)." Jews of Lviv archive. https://europebetweeneastandwest.wordpress.com/tag/jews-of-lviv/.

Journeyman Pictures. 2012. "The Last Generation – Poland." www.youtube.com/watch?v=i2hCH5ANJBE.

Kessler, Edmund. 2010. The Wartime Diary of Edmund Kessler, Lwow, Poland, 1942–1944. Edited by Renata Kessler. Academic Studies Press.

Landfried, Jessica. 2002 (June). "Brief History of the City of Lviv." UCSB Oral History Project: Resources. www.history.ucsb.edu/projects/holocaust/Resources/history_of_lviv.htm.

Peltz, Diana. "Central State Historical Archives of Ukraine in Lviv." Lviv Historical Archives. Roots to Roots Foundation. www.rtrfoundation.org/webart/UkraineChapters-Peltz.pdf.

Stewart, Will. 2015 (August 24). "The Secrets of Ukraine's Shameful 'Holocaust of Bullets' Killing Centre where 1.6 Million Jews Were Executed." Daily Mail online. www.dailymail.co.uk/news/article-3205754/Blood-oozed-soil-grave-sites-pits-alive-secrets-Ukraine-s-shameful-Holocaust-Bullets-killing-centre-1-6million-Jews-executed.html.

Wikipedia. 2017. "Bełżec Extermination Camp." https://en.m.wikipedia.org/wiki/Be%C5%82%C5%BCec_extermination_camp.

Wikipedia. 2017 (March 7). "Lwów Ghetto." https://en.wikipedia.org/wiki/Lw%C3%B3w_Ghetto.

Brussels, 1943–1944

Beyer, John C., and Stephen A. Schneider. 1999. "Forced Labor Under the Third Reich." Two-part study. Nathan Associates Inc. www.nathaninc.com/resources/forced-labor-under-third-reich.

JDC (American Jewish Joint Distribution Committee). "Report on Belgian Jews." Archive Document. http://search.archives.jdc.org/multimedia/Documents/NY_AR3344/33-44_Count_1/AR33-44_Count_05/NY_AR3344_Count_05_00608.pdf.

Pagenstecher, Cord. 2010. " 'We Were Treated Like Slaves.' Remembering Forced Labor for Nazi Germany." In G. Mackenthun and R. Hormann (eds.), Human Bondage in the Cultural Contact Zone. Transdisciplinary Perspectives on Slavery and Its Discourses. Munster, pp. 275–291. www.cord-pagenstecher.de/pagenstecher-2010b-treated-like-slaves.htm.

The Tide Turns: Brussels, 1944

Tenenbaum, Marcel. 2016. Of Men, Monsters and Mazel: Surviving the Final Solution in Belgium. Xlibris.

After Liberation

Jewish refugees during and after the war:

Gruber, Ruth. 2007. *Witness: One of the Great Foreign Correspondents of the Twentieth Century Tells Her Story.* Schocken Books. See especially Chapters 4, 5, and 6.

Palmyam. "The Voyage of the 'Theodor Herzl'." www.palyam.org/English/Hahapala/hf/hf_Theodor_Herzl.

Scrapbookpages.com. 2010 (January 27). "The Deportation of the Hungarian Jews."

HungarianJews.html.

The Cyprus internment camps:

Palmyam. "The Cyprus Detention Camps." www.palyam.org/English/Arrests/hfCyprus.

Shoah Resource Center. "Cyprus Detention Camps." The International School for Holocaust Studies. Yad Vashem. www.yadvashem.org/odot_pdf/Microsoft%20Word%20-%20727.pdf.

Wikipedia. 2017 (March 18). "Cyprus Internment Camps." https://en.wikipedia.org/wiki/Cyprus_internment_camps.

The British Mandate in Palestine:

For Critical Thinkers. 2015. "IsraelPalestine for Critical Thinkers: #8 – The British Mandate." www.youtube.com/watch?v=Y3_5nTRuoO8.

Toldot Yisrael. 2015. "By Air, Land, and Sea: Aliyah under the British Mandate." www.youtube.com/watch?v=boqviMZ4urg.

Reflections on a Calamity

JDC (American Jewish Joint Distribution Committee) website. www.jdc.org.

Epigenetics and the transmission of trauma to future generations:

Carey, Nessa. 2012. The Epigenetic Revolution: How Modern Biology is Rewriting Our Understanding of Genetics, Disease, and Inheritance. Columbia University Press.

Francis, Richard C. 2011. Epigenetics: How Environment Shapes Our Genes. W.W. Norton & Company.

Kellerman, Natan P.F. "Transmission of Holocaust Trauma." AMCHA – National Israeli Center for Psychosocial Support of Survivors of the Holocaust and the Second Generation. Published in 2013 as "Epigenetic Transmission of Holocaust Trauma: Can Nightmares Be Inherited?" Israeli Journal of Psychiatry and Related Sciences 50(1).

Mansuy, Isabelle M., and Safa Mohanna. 2001 (May 25). "Epigenetics and the Human Brain." The Dana Foundation.

http://dana.org/Cerebrum/2011/Epigenetics_and_the_Human_Brain__Where_Nurture_Meets_Nature/.

Moalem, Sharon. 2014. Inheritance: How Our Genes Change Our Lives and Our Lives Change Our Genes. Grand Central Publishing.

Rodriguez, Tori. 2015 (March 1). "Descendants of Holocaust Survivors Have Altered Stress Hormones." Scientific American.

www.scientificamerican.com/article/descendants-of-holocaust-survivors-have-altered-stress-hormones/.

Shulevitz, Judith. 2014 (November 16). "The Science of Suffering: Kids Are Inheriting Their Parents' Trauma. Can Science Stop It?" New Republic. https://newrepublic.com/article/120144/trauma-genetic-scientists-say-parents-are-passing-ptsd-kids.

Thompson, Helen. 2015 (August 21). "Study of Holocaust Survivors Finds Trauma Passed On to Children's Genes." The Guardian. www.theguardian.com/science/2015/aug/21/study-of-holocaust-survivors-finds-trauma-passed-on-to-childrens-genes.

Yehuda, Rachel. 2015 (July 30). "How Trauma and Resilience Cross Generations." On Being. https://onbeing.org/programs/rachel-yehuda-how-trauma-and-resilience-cross-generations/.

Yehuda, Rachel, Nikolaos P. Daskalakis, Linda M. Bierer, Heather N. Bader, Torsten Klengel, Florian Holsboer, and Elisabeth B. Binder. 2016 (September 1). "Holocaust Exposure Induced Intergenerational Effects on FKBP5 Methylation." Biological Psychiatry 80(5). www.biologicalpsychiatryjournal.com/article/S0006-3223(15)00652-6/abstract.

Zhao, Roseanne. 2013 (July 3). "Child Abuse Leaves Epigenetic Marks." National Human Genome Research Institute. www.genome.gov/27554258/child-abuse-leaves-epigenetic-marks/

What made the Holocaust possible?

McLeod, Saul. 2008, updated 2016. "Stanford Prison Experiment." Simply Psychology. www.simplypsychology.org/zimbardo.html.

Children's experience of the Holocaust:

Silberman, Lili. 2015. "Beyond Secret Tears." Anti-Defamation League. www.adl.org/sites/default/files/documents/assets/pdf/education-outreach/children-of-the-holocaust-discussion-guide-beyond-secret-tears.pdf.

On Israel:

Center for Israel Education. 2016. "Immigration." https://israeled.org/themes/immigration/.

JTA. 2015 (May 8). "Israel and Germany Mark 50 Years of Diplomatic Relations." The Jerusalem Post. www.jpost.com/Israel-News/Israel-and-Germany-mark-golden-anniversary-as-friends-402475.

Dear Reader

Having written these memoirs means a lot to me, and I feel grateful for the many positive comments it has received so far. Reviews are the most powerful when it comes to getting attention for a book. Honest reviews of my books help me getting more attention for what I write.

If you've enjoyed this book I would be very grateful if you could spend a few minutes leaving a review (it can be as short as you like) on the Amazon page. You can jump right there to the page by clicking below:

My Book on Amazon.com
My Book on Amazon.co.uk

Thanks a lot in advance!

Tammy Bottner

AMSTERDAM PUBLISHERS HOLOCAUST LIBRARY

The series **Holocaust Survivor Memoirs World War II** consists of the following autobiographies of survivors:

Outcry. Holocaust Memoirs, by Manny Steinberg

Hank Brodt Holocaust Memoirs. A Candle and a Promise, by Deborah Donnelly

The Dead Years. Holocaust Memoirs, by Joseph Schupack

Rescued from the Ashes. The Diary of Leokadia Schmidt, Survivor of the Warsaw Ghetto, by Leokadia Schmidt

My Lvov. Holocaust Memoir of a twelve-year-old Girl, by Janina Hescheles

Remembering Ravensbrück. From Holocaust to Healing, by Natalie Hess

Wolf. A Story of Hate, by Zeev Scheinwald with Ella Scheinwald

Save my Children. An Astonishing Tale of Survival and its Unlikely Hero, by Leon Kleiner with Edwin Stepp

Holocaust Memoirs of a Bergen-Belsen Survivor & Classmate of Anne Frank, by Nanette Blitz Konig

Defiant German - Defiant Jew. A Holocaust Memoir from inside the Third Reich, by Walter Leopold with Les Leopold

In a Land of Forest and Darkness. The Holocaust Story of two Jewish Partisans, by Sara Lustigman Omelinski

Holocaust Memories. Annihilation and Survival in Slovakia, by Paul
Davidovits

From Auschwitz with Love. The Inspiring Memoir of Two Sisters'
Survival, Devotion and Triumph Told by Manci Grunberger Beran &
Ruth Grunberger Mermelstein, by Daniel Seymour

Remetz. Resistance Fighter and Survivor of the Warsaw Ghetto, by Jan
Yohay Remetz

My March Through Hell. A Young Girl's Terrifying Journey to Survival,
by Halina Kleiner with Edwin Stepp

Roman's Journey, by Roman Halter

Memoirs by Elmar Rivosh, Sculptor (1906-1967). Riga Ghetto and
Beyond, by Elmar Rivosh

The series **Holocaust Survivor True Stories WWII** consists of the
following biographies:

Among the Reeds. The true story of how a family survived the Holocaust,
by Tammy Bottner

A Holocaust Memoir of Love & Resilience. Mama's Survival from
Lithuania to America, by Ettie Zilber

Living among the Dead. My Grandmother's Holocaust Survival Story of
Love and Strength, by Adena Bernstein Astrowsky

Heart Songs. A Holocaust Memoir, by Barbara Gilford

Shoes of the Shoah. The Tomorrow of Yesterday, by Dorothy Pierce

Hidden in Berlin. A Holocaust Memoir, by Evelyn Joseph Grossman

Separated Together. The Incredible True WWII Story of Soulmates Stranded an Ocean Apart, by Kenneth P. Price, Ph.D.

The Man Across the River. The incredible story of one man's will to survive the Holocaust, by Zvi Wiesenfeld

If Anyone Calls, Tell Them I Died. A Memoir, by Emanuel (Manu) Rosen

The House on Thrömerstrasse. A Story of Rebirth and Renewal in the Wake of the Holocaust, by Ron Vincent

Dancing with my Father. His hidden past. Her quest for truth. How Nazi Vienna shaped a family's identity, by Jo Sorochinsky

The Story Keeper. Weaving the Threads of Time and Memory - A Memoir, by Fred Feldman

Krisia's Silence. The Girl who was not on Schindler's List, by Ronny Hein

Defying Death on the Danube. A Holocaust Survival Story, by Debbie J. Callahan with Henry Stern

A Doorway to Heroism. A decorated German-Jewish Soldier who became an American Hero, by Rabbi W. Jack Romberg

The Shoemaker's Son. The Life of a Holocaust Resister, by Laura Beth Bakst

The Redhead of Auschwitz. A True Story, by Nechama Birnbaum

Land of Many Bridges. My Father's Story, by Bela Ruth Samuel Tenenholtz

Creating Beauty from the Abyss. The Amazing Story of Sam Herciger, Auschwitz Survivor and Artist, by Lesley Ann Richardson

On Sunny Days We Sang. A Holocaust Story of Survival and Resilience, by Jeannette Grunhaus de Gelman

Painful Joy. A Holocaust Family Memoir, by Max J. Friedman

I Give You My Heart. A True Story of Courage and Survival, by Wendy Holden

In the Time of Madmen, by Mark A. Prelas

Monsters and Miracles. Horror, Heroes and the Holocaust, by Ira Wesley Kitmacher

Flower of Vlora. Growing up Jewish in Communist Albania, by Anna Kohen

Aftermath: Coming of Age on Three Continents. A Memoir, by Annette Libeskind Berkovits

Not a real Enemy. The True Story of a Hungarian Jewish Man's Fight for Freedom, by Robert Wolf

Zaidy's War. Four Armies, Three Continents, Two Brothers. One Man's Impossible Story of Endurance, by Martin Bodek

The Glassmaker's Son. Looking for the World my Father left behind in Nazi Germany, by Peter Kupfer

The Apprentice of Buchenwald. The True Story of the Teenage Boy Who Sabotaged Hitler's War Machine, by Oren Schneider

Burying the Ghosts, by Sonia Case

American Wolf. From Nazi Refugee to American Spy. A True Story, by Audrey Birnbaum

Bipolar Refugee. A Saga of Survival and Resilience, by Peter Wiesner

---

The series **Jewish Children in the Holocaust** consists of the following autobiographies of Jewish children hidden during WWII in the Netherlands:

Searching for Home. The Impact of WWII on a Hidden Child, by Joseph Gosler

See You Tonight and Promise to be a Good Boy! War memories, by Salo Muller

Sounds from Silence. Reflections of a Child Holocaust Survivor, Psychiatrist and Teacher, by Robert Krell

Sabine's Odyssey. A Hidden Child and her Dutch Rescuers, by Agnes Schipper

The Journey of a Hidden Child, by Harry Pila and Robin Black

The series **New Jewish Fiction** consists of the following novels, written by Jewish authors. All novels are set in the time during or after the Holocaust.

The Corset Maker. A Novel, by Annette Libeskind Berkovits

Escaping the Whale. The Holocaust is over. But is it ever over for the next generation? by Ruth Rotkowitz

When the Music Stopped. Willy Rosen's Holocaust, by Casey Hayes

Hands of Gold. One Man's Quest to Find the Silver Lining in Misfortune, by Roni Robbins

The Girl Who Counted Numbers. A Novel, by Roslyn Bernstein

There was a garden in Nuremberg. A Novel, by Navina Michal Clemerson

The Butterfly and the Axe, by Omer Bartov

To Live Another Day. A Novel, Elizabeth Rosenberg

A Worthy Life. A Novel, by Dahlia Moore

Good for a Single Journey, by Helen Joyce

The series **Holocaust Heritage** consists of the following memoirs by 2G:

The Cello Still Sings. A Generational Story of the Holocaust and of the Transformative Power of Music, by Janet Horvath

The Silk Factory: Finding Threads of My Family's True Holocaust Story, by Michael Hickins

The Fire and the Bonfire. A Journey into Memory, by Ardyn Halter

---

The series **Holocaust Books for Young Adults** consists of the following novels, based on true stories:

The Boy behind the Door. How Salomon Kool Escaped the Nazis. Inspired by a True Story, by David Tabatsky

Running for Shelter. A True Story, by Suzette Sheft

The Precious Few. An Inspirational Saga of Courage based on True Stories, by David Twain with Art Twain

Jacob's Courage: A Holocaust Love Story, by Charles S. Weinblatt

---

The series **WW2 Historical Fiction** consists of the following novels, some of which are based on true stories:

Mendelevski's Box. A Heartwarming and Heartbreaking Jewish Survivor's Story, by Roger Swindells

A Quiet Genocide. The Untold Holocaust of Disabled Children WW2 Germany, by Glenn Bryant

The Knife-Edge Path, by Patrick T. Leahy

Brave Face. The Inspiring WWII Memoir of a Dutch/German Child, by I. Caroline Crocker and Meta A. Evenbly

When We Had Wings. The Gripping Story of an Orphan in Janusz Korczak's Orphanage. A Historical Novel, by Tami Shem-Tov

Want to be an AP book reviewer?

Reviews are very important in a world dominated by the social media and social proof. Please drop us a line if you want to join the *AP review team* and show us at least one review already posted on Amazon for one of our books. info@amsterdampublishers.com

Printed in Great Britain
by Amazon

21987440R10155